本書の構成と利用法

それぞれのパートは見開き 2 ページで構成されています。

見開きの左ページ

A 新出単語を主な対象として，単語の意味もしくは英語を書かせる問題です。
A1〜B2は，CEFR-J でのレベルを表します。A1（易）〜B2（難）です。

B 新出単語を主な対象とした発音問題もしくはアクセント問題です。

C 重要な表現や文法に関する空所補充問題です。

D 重要な表現や文法に関する語句整序問題です。

見開きの右ページ

E 教科書本文の理解を確認する問題です。適語選択や語形変化，語句整序，英問英答など，多様な形式の問題を用意しました。

『CEFR-J Wordlist Version 1.6』東京外国語大学投野由紀夫研究室．（URL: http://cefr-j.org/download.html より2021年2月ダウンロード）

A Translate the English into Japanese and the Japanese into English. 【語彙の知識】(各1点)

1. .... 形 B2　影響力を持つ　　2. icon 名 B2　　　　　[　　　　　　]

3. .... 形　　大げさな, オーバーな　4. imitation 名 B2　[　　　　　　]

5. praise 動 B2　　[　　　　　]　　6. .... 動 B1　…を手に入れる, …を得る

B Choose the word whose underlined part is pronounced differently from the other three.【発音の知識】(各2点)

1. ア. entert<u>ai</u>nment　　イ. g<u>ai</u>n　　　　ウ. pr<u>ai</u>se　　　エ. s<u>ai</u>d

2. ア. con<u>f</u>idence　　　イ. <u>i</u>con　　　　ウ. <u>i</u>nterview　　エ. m<u>i</u>llion

3. ア. bec<u>a</u>me　　　　　イ. ex<u>a</u>ggerated　ウ. <u>i</u>mitation　　エ. l<u>a</u>dy

C Complete the following English sentences to match the Japanese.【表現と文法の知識】

(各3点)

1. そのようにして私は妻と出会った。

(　　　　　　) (　　　　　　　　) I met my wife.

2. 物まねとは, 誰かの言葉や行動をまねることです。

(　　　　　　　) is an attempt to copy someone's words and actions.

3. 彼はキャプテンとしてチームで影響力のある役割を果たした。

He played an (　　　　　　) (　　　　　　　) as captain on the team.

D Arrange the words in the proper order to match the Japanese.【表現と文法の知識・技能】

(各3点)

1. 先生はその生徒の努力をほめた。

Our teacher (for / his hard work / praised / the student).

2. その少女が見つけた昆虫は, 新種として認められた。

The insect the girl found (a new species / as / recognized / was).

3. 母はいつも私に自分らしさを大事にしなさいと言う。

My mother always tells me to (am / I / treasure / who).

E Read the following passage and answer the questions below.

Naomi Watanabe is one of the most influential stars on social media. Now she is recognized as an international fashion icon and (1)(follow) by about 10 million fans. She started her career (2) a comedian in 2007. She became popular for her exaggerated imitations of Beyoncé and Lady Gaga. In 2019, she moved to New York to improve her career.

Foreign media praise Naomi (3) her style in the fields of entertainment and fashion. Once she said in an interview, "I (4)(people / to / treasure / want / who) they are — that's how I gained confidence. I want (5)(love / tell / them / to / to) themselves."

1. 下線部(1)の語を適切な形に変えなさい。【語彙と文法の知識】　　　　　　　　　　(2 点)

　　..

2. 空所(2), (3)に入る最も適当な語を選びなさい。【語彙の知識】　　　　　　　　(各 2 点)
　　(2) ア. as　　　　　イ. for　　　　　ウ. in　　　　　エ. to
　　(3) ア. as　　　　　イ. by　　　　　ウ. for　　　　　エ. to

3. 下線部(4), (5)の(　　)内の語を適切に並べかえなさい。【表現と文法の知識】　　(各 3 点)
　　(4) ....
　　(5) ....

4. 次の問いに英語で答えなさい。【内容についての思考力・判断力・表現力】　　　　(各 4 点)
　　(1) What made Naomi popular?

　　..
　　(2) Why did Naomi move to New York in 2019?

　　..

A Translate the English into Japanese and the Japanese into English.【語彙の知識】（各1点）

1. .... 名 B2　探検家
2. creature 名 A2　[　　　　　]
3. .... 動 B2　…に近づく
4. designate 動　[　　　　　]
5. .... 形 A2　絶滅の危機に瀕した
6. disappointed 形 A2　[　　　　　]

B Choose the word which has primary stress on a different syllable from the other three.【アクセントの知識】（各2点）

1. ア. crea-ture　　イ. im-prove　　ウ. is-land　　エ. main-land
2. ア. des-ig-nate　イ. dis-cov-er　ウ. en-dan-gered　エ. how-ev-er
3. ア. co-me-di-an　イ. dis-ap-point-ed　ウ. en-ter-tain-ment　エ. in-flu-en-tial

C Complete the following English sentences to match the Japanese.【表現と文法の知識】

（各3点）

1. トラは絶滅危惧種である。

Tigers are an (　　　　　) (　　　　　).

2. この試験では辞書を用いてもよい。

You (　　　　　) (　　　　　) (　　　　　) use your dictionary on this test.

3. たとえ結果が悪くてもがっかりしてはいけないよ。

Even if the result is bad, (　　　　　) (　　　　　) (　　　　　).

D Arrange the words in the proper order to match the Japanese.【表現と文法の知識・技能】

（各3点）

1. ユキはチームのキャプテンに指名されて驚いた。

Yuki was surprised (as / be / designated / to) captain of the team.

2. 小笠原諸島固有の昆虫がたくさんいます。

There are many insects (are / native / that / to) the Ogasawara Islands.

3. 寒い朝は，温かい味噌汁を食べるだけで幸せな気持ちになる。

On cold mornings, (happy / just eating / makes / me / warm miso soup).

E Read the following passage and answer the questions below.

You (1)(animals / know / may / some / that) — koalas, kangaroos and wombats — are native to Australia. But, how about quokkas? (2) their round cheeks and cute smiles, they are called "the happiest animals on earth."

Quokkas mainly live on Rottnest Island in the southwest of the Australian mainland. The name "Rottnest" comes (3) the Dutch phrase for "rat's nest." When they were first discovered by Dutch explorers in the 17th century, (4)they were mistaken for giant rats.

Quokkas (5)(are / creatures / friendly / such / that) they approach tourists for food. However, they are designated as an endangered species, so you are not allowed to touch or feed them. But don't be disappointed. Just looking at their smiles will make you happy.

1. 下線部(1)，(5)の(　　)内の語を適切に並べかえなさい。【表現の知識】　　　（各3点）

　(1)　_____

　(5)　_____

2. 空所(2)，(3)に入る最も適当な語(句)を選びなさい。【語彙と表現の知識】　　　（各2点）

　(2) ア. As for　　　イ. Instead of　　　ウ. Thanks to　　　エ. Without

　(3) ア. as　　　イ. from　　　ウ. in　　　エ. to

3. 下線部(4)の they が指すものを，本文中より抜き出しなさい。

【内容についての思考力・判断力・表現力】（2点）

　_____

4. 次の問いに英語で答えなさい。【内容についての思考力・判断力・表現力】　　　（各4点）

　(1) What are quokkas called?

　_____

　(2) Are tourists allowed to feed quokkas?

　_____

A Translate the English into Japanese and the Japanese into English.【語彙の知識】（各1点）

1. ＿＿＿＿＿＿＿＿ 名　彫刻家　　　　2. overflow 動　[　　　　　　　]

3. severely 副 B1　[　　　　　]　　　4. ＿＿＿＿＿＿ 動 A2　…を批判する

5. reflect 動 A2　[　　　　　]　　　6. ＿＿＿＿＿＿ 動 B1　…を落胆させる

B Choose the word which has primary stress on a different syllable from the other three.【アクセントの知識】

(各2点)

1. ア. al-low　　　イ. ap-proach　　　ウ. chal-lenge　　　エ. re-flect

2. ア. at-ti-tude　　イ. con-sid-er　　　ウ. dis-cour-age　　エ. se-vere-ly

3. ア. con-sis-tent　イ. crit-i-cize　　　ウ. mon-u-ment　　エ. prim-i-tive

C Complete the following English sentences to match the Japanese.【表現と文法の知識】（各3点）

1. 私は会ったことがないので，彼のことは全然知りません。

I have never met him, so I don't know him (　　　　　) (　　　　　).

2. 口を食べ物でいっぱいにして話すのは不作法だとみなされている国もある。

It is (　　　　　) bad manners in some countries to speak with your mouth full of food.

3. 彼女は仕事に対する態度がとても前向きである。

She has a very positive (　　　　　) toward her work.

D Arrange the words in the proper order to match the Japanese.【表現と文法の知識・技能】

(各3点)

1. ファン・ゴッホの「ひまわり」は，世界で最も有名な絵画のひとつである。

Van Gogh's "Sunflowers" is (famous / most / of / one / paintings / the) in the world.

＿＿＿＿＿＿＿＿＿＿＿＿＿＿＿＿＿＿＿＿＿＿＿＿＿＿＿

2. 計画は変更されたが，その理由は誰も知らないようだ。

The plan has been changed, but (know / nobody / seems / the reason / to) for it.

＿＿＿＿＿＿＿＿＿＿＿＿＿＿＿＿＿＿＿＿＿＿＿＿＿＿＿

3. 子供は挿絵がたくさんついている本が好きだ。

Children like (books / illustrations / lots / of / with).

＿＿＿＿＿＿＿＿＿＿＿＿＿＿＿＿＿＿＿＿＿＿＿＿＿＿＿

E Read the following passage and answer the questions below.

Do you know of Taro Okamoto, (1) was one of the most famous Japanese artists? (2) a painter, sculptor and writer, he challenged traditional Japanese values.

(2) a producer of Expo '70, Okamoto created *the Tower of the Sun*, a monument overflowing with primitive power. At that time, it was severely criticized by some artists because it didn't seem to reflect the traditional Japanese sense of beauty. (3), (4)such criticism didn't discourage him at all. He was an artist with a consistent attitude and strong beliefs. (5)Now *the Tower of the Sun* is considered one of his most outstanding works.

1. 空所(1)~(3)に入る最も適当な語を選びなさい。【表現と文法の知識】　　　(各2点)
   (1) ア. it　　　　　イ. he　　　　　ウ. who　　　　　エ. which
   (2) ア. As　　　　イ. By　　　　　ウ. For　　　　　エ. Like
   (3) ア. Also　　　イ. Instead　　　ウ. So　　　　　エ. Yet

2. 下線部(4)とは具体的にどのような批判ですか。日本語で答えなさい。
   【内容についての思考力・判断力・表現力】（3点）

3. 下線部(5)と対照的に用いられている語句を，本文中から抜き出しなさい。【語彙と表現の知識】
   （3点）

4. 次の問いに英語で答えなさい。【内容についての思考力・判断力・表現力】　　　(各4点)
   (1) Why was Okamoto not at all discouraged by criticism from some artists?

   (2) How is *the Tower of the Sun* considered today?

A Translate the English into Japanese and the Japanese into English.【語彙の知識】（各1点）

1. ＿＿＿＿＿＿＿ 名 B2　発明家
2. detect 動 B2　[　　　　　　　]
3. cyberbullying 名　[　　　　　　　]
4. ＿＿＿＿＿＿＿ 名　汚染
5. ＿＿＿＿＿＿＿ 形 B2　革新的な
6. tackle 動 B2　[　　　　　　　]

B Choose the word whose underlined part is pronounced differently from the other three.【発音の知識】（各2点）

1. ア. detect　　イ. identify　　ウ. inventor　　エ. mission
2. ア. approach　イ. contamination　ウ. exaggerated　エ. tackle
3. ア. consider　イ. device　　ウ. icon　　エ. kindly

C Complete the following English sentences to match the Japanese.【表現と文法の知識】（各3点）

1. 彼は16歳から働き始めました。

   He started to work at (　　　　　) (　　　　　) (　　　　　) 16.

2. 医者は，私の頭痛は明かりが十分でないところで本を読んでいることに関連があると言っている。

   My doctor says my headaches are (　　　　　) (　　　　　) reading in poorly lit areas.

3. 準備の良し悪しで最終的な結果が大きく変わる。

   Good preparation makes a big (　　　　　) in the final result.

D Arrange the words in the proper order to match the Japanese.【表現と文法の知識・技能】（各3点）

1. ラッセルという人から電話ですよ。

   There is (called / on / Russell / someone / the phone).

2. 学ぶのに遅すぎるということはない。（ことわざ）

   It's (late / learn / never / to / too).

3. 試験の問題の全部に答える時間は十分にありましたか。

   Did you have (all / answer / enough time / on / the questions / to) the exam?

E Read the following passage and answer the questions below.

Gitanjali Rao was selected as *TIME*'s 2020 "Kid of the Year" at the age of 15. The Indian-American scientist and inventor uses technology to solve social and environmental problems.

(1), Gitanjali invented an AI-based service called "Kindly." It detects words that could be related to cyberbullying. She also (2)created "Tethys," a device that can identify lead contamination in drinking water.

Her mission doesn't stop there. Gitanjali has also held innovative workshops on STEM globally. With these workshops, she intends (3) a global community of young innovators (4) world problems. She says, "It's never too early (5) making a difference. Every one of us has the power (6) the world."

1. 空所(1)に入る最も適当な語句を選びなさい。【語彙と表現の知識】 （2点）

　　ア. As a result　　イ. For example　　ウ. However　　エ. In addition

2. 下線部(2)の created に最も近い意味を表す語を，本文中から1語で抜き出しなさい。

【語彙の知識】（2点）

　　(　　　　　　　)

3. 空所(3)〜(6)に入る最も適当な語句をそれぞれ選びなさい。

【内容についての思考力・判断力・表現力】（各2点）

　　ア. to change　　イ. to create　　ウ. to start　　エ. to tackle

　　(3) (　　)　　　　(4) (　　)　　　　(5) (　　)　　　　(6) (　　)

4. 次の問いに英語で答えなさい。【内容についての思考力・判断力・表現力】 （各4点）

　　(1) With an AI-based service called "Kindly," what can we do?

　　────────────────────────────

　　(2) Gitanjali created a device called "Tethys." What can the device do?

　　────────────────────────────

A Translate the English into Japanese and the Japanese into English.【語彙の知識】(各1点)

1. _____ 名　比, 比率
2. architectural 形　[　　　　　　　　]
3. compose 動 B1　[　　　　　　　　]
4. _____ 副　本能的に, 直感的に
5. _____ 形 B2　バランスのとれた
6. pleasing 形 A2　[　　　　　　　　]

B Choose the word whose underlined part is pronounced differently from the other three.【発音の知識】 (各2点)

1. ア. A<u>th</u>ens　　イ. <u>b</u>alance　　ウ. <u>n</u>ational　　エ. ra<u>t</u>io
2. ア. pl<u>ea</u>sing　　イ. rel<u>ea</u>se　　ウ. s<u>ea</u>shell　　エ. spr<u>ea</u>d
3. ア. ar<u>ch</u>itectural　　イ. <u>ch</u>arity　　ウ. <u>ch</u>oose　　エ. handker<u>ch</u>ief

C Complete the following English sentences to match the Japanese.【表現と文法の知識】(各3点)

1. イギリスに行ったとき, 有名な都市を訪れました。たとえばロンドンやリバプールのような。

   When I traveled to the UK, I visited some famous cities. (　　　　　　　　)
   (　　　　　　　　), I went to London and Liverpool.

2. 私を含めて4人が会議に参加します。

   Four people, (　　　　　　　　) me, will take part in the meeting.

3. 私の息子はトマトやブロッコリーのような野菜が大好きです。

   My son really likes vegetables, (　　　　　　　　) (　　　　　　　　) tomatoes and broccoli.

D Arrange the words in the proper order to match the Japanese.【表現と文法の知識・技能】

(各3点)

1. たくさんの人が彼女の他人への優しさにひかれる。

   Many people (are / attracted / her kindness / to / toward) others.

   _____

2. ここの人は観光客に優しいと言われている。

   (is / it / said / that) people here are kind to tourists.

   _____

3. 今朝からおなかが痛いのです。昨日刺し身を食べたからかもしれません。

   I have had a stomachache since this morning. (be / because / it / may) I had sashimi yesterday.

   _____

E Read the following passage and answer the questions below.

Look at these pictures. They all have the "golden ratio" in them. The golden ratio is a mathematical ratio of 1:1.618.

It is said that many famous architectural works, artworks and other objects have been (1)(compose) with this ratio. (2), the Pyramids of Giza in Egypt, the Parthenon in Athens, and Kinkakuji Temple in Kyoto are among them.

(3)(are / attracted / people / to / why) these structures? It may be (4)(a / kind / because / is / of / the golden ratio) law and order of nature. We can also find the golden ratio in beautiful objects in nature, (5) flowers, ferns and seashells. When we see objects with this ratio, we instinctively feel that they are well-balanced, pleasing and beautiful.

1. 下線部(1)の語を適切な形に変えなさい。【語彙と文法の知識】　　　　　　　　　　（2点）

2. 空所(2), (5)に入る最も適当な語（句）を選びなさい。【語彙と表現の知識】　　　　（各2点）
 (2) ア. As a result イ. Besides ウ. For example エ. Such as
 (5) ア. and   イ. or   ウ. such as   エ. that

3. 下線部(3), (4)の（　　）内の語句を適切に並べかえなさい。【表現の知識】　　　（各3点）
 (3)
 (4)

4. 次の問いに英語で答えなさい。【内容についての思考力・判断力・表現力】　　　（各4点）
 (1) What is the golden ratio?

 (2) How do we feel when we see objects with the golden ratio?

A Translate the English into Japanese and the Japanese into English.【語彙の知識】（各1点）

1. _____ 形　倫理的な，道徳的な　2. consumption 名 B1　[　　　　　　　]

3. _____ 名 B1　考慮，配慮　　　4. consumer 名 B1　[　　　　　　　]

5. install 動 B1　[　　　　　　　]　　6. _____ 形 A2　電動の，電気の

B Choose the word which has primary stress on a different syllable from the other three.【アクセントの知識】 （各2点）

1. ア. con-sume　　　イ. in-stall　　　ウ. pro-duce　　　エ. prod-uct

2. ア. ap-pli-ance　　イ. con-sum-er　　ウ. e-lec-tric　　エ. eth-i-cal

3. ア. ar-chi-tec-tur-al　イ. con-sid-er-a-tion　ウ. in-ter-na-tion-al　エ. math-e-mat-i-cal

C Complete the following English sentences to match the Japanese.【表現と文法の知識】

（各3点）

1. この県は，日本一のうどんの消費量を誇っている。

This prefecture has the highest (　　　　　　　) of udon in Japan.

2. 洗濯機を取り付けるだけで多くの費用がかかる。

Just (　　　　　　　) a washing machine costs a lot of money.

3. これらすべての電化製品の利用が毎月の家賃に含まれています。

Use of all these (　　　　　　) (　　　　　　　) are included in the monthly rent.

D Arrange the words in the proper order to match the Japanese.【表現と文法の知識・技能】

（各3点）

1. 春がもうすぐそこまで来ている。

Spring (around / is / just / the corner).

_____

2. イチゴやミカンのような甘酸っぱい果物が食べたい。

I want to (as / eat / fruits / such / sweet-and-sour) strawberries and oranges.

_____

3. 新しい道路は，地域の住民の生活に配慮して建設されなければならない。

New roads must be constructed (consideration / in / lives / of / the local people's).

_____

E Read the following passage and answer the questions below.

Have you ever heard of "ethical consumption"? It means to choose products or services in consideration of the environment, human rights, or animal welfare.

(1) can we become ethical consumers? For example, we can choose ethical products such as fair-trade, eco-friendly or (2)(recycle) products. When shopping, it is important to consider how the products were produced before buying them. (3)(can / choosing / ethical / help / products / to) improve our society.

We can also (4)(by / help / save / the environment / to) installing solar panels or choosing electric appliances with low power consumption. The time is just around the corner (5) it will be normal to live as an ethical consumer.

1. 空所(1)に入る最も適当な語を選びなさい。【語彙の知識】　(2点)

　　ア. How　　　　イ. What　　　　ウ. Where　　　　エ. Who

2. 下線部(2)の語を適切な形に変えなさい。【語彙の知識】　(2点)

　　..

3. 下線部(3), (4)の(　　)内の語句を適切に並べかえなさい。【表現と文法の知識】　(各3点)

　　(3) ....

　　(4) ....

4. 空所(5)に入る最も適当な語を選びなさい。【文法の知識】　(2点)

　　ア. what　　　　イ. when　　　　ウ. where　　　　エ. which

5. 次の問いに英語で答えなさい。【内容についての思考力・判断力・表現力】　(各4点)

　　(1) What does "ethical consumption" mean?

　　..

　　(2) What should we consider when shopping?

　　..

Get Ready

A Translate the English into Japanese and the Japanese into English. 【語彙の知識】 (各1点)

1. ＿＿＿＿＿＿＿＿ 名 A2 孤児　　　　　2. wilderness 名 B2　　[　　　　　　　　]

3. survival 名 B1　　[　　　　　　　]　　4. ＿＿＿＿＿＿＿＿ 形　丈夫な，頑丈な

5. ＿＿＿＿＿＿＿＿ 動 B2 …を割る，…を砕く　6. illegal 形 A2　　[　　　　　　　　]

B Choose the word which has primary stress on a different syllable from the other three. 【アクセントの知識】　　　　　　　　　　　　　　　　　　　　　　　(各2点)

1. ア. ca-reer　　　イ. de-stroy　　　ウ. re-sult　　　エ. stur-dy

2. ア. des-ig-nate　　イ. in-ter-view　　ウ. rec-og-nize　　エ. sur-viv-al

3. ア. con-fi-dence　　イ. eth-i-cal　　ウ. il-le-gal　　エ. wil-der-ness

C Complete the following English sentences to match the Japanese. 【表現と文法の知識】

(各3点)

1. その会社の新しい事務所は郊外にある。

The company's new office is (　　　　　　) outside the city.

2. その古代都市は砂漠の砂の下に埋没してしまう危機に瀕しています。

The ancient city is (　　　　　) (　　　　　　) (　　　　　　) disappearing under the sands of the desert.

3. 日本の伝統的な美意識をどう思いますか。

(　　　　　　) do you think about the traditional Japanese sense of beauty?

D Arrange the words in the proper order to match the Japanese. 【表現と文法の知識・技能】

(各3点)

1. 彼女が誰にもさよならを言わないで去って行ったのにはびっくりしました。

I was surprised that she left (anyone / goodbye / saying / to / without).

2. 私はこんなふうに扱われることに慣れていません。

I'm not used (being / like / this / to / treated).

3. 自分のお小遣いをどう使うか決めるのは子供にまかせるべきだ。

Children should be allowed to (decide / how / spend / their pocket money / to).

E Read the following passage and answer the questions below.

Do you know there are some jungle schools for orangutans? These unique schools to protect them are located in a jungle in Borneo, Indonesia.

The orangutans at these schools have been left orphans. They can't live in the real wilderness without first being taught (1)survival skills by humans. That's (2) they are learning how to build sturdy nests, how to crack coconuts, and even how to climb trees.

Orangutans are losing their homes because their rainforest habitat (3) due to human activities such as plantation development and illegal deforestation. (4), they are in danger of extinction. What do you think about (5)the selfishness of human beings?

1. 下線部(1)は具体的にどのような技能ですか。日本語で答えなさい。
【内容についての思考力・判断力・表現力】(3 点)

2. 空所(2), (3), (4)に入る最も適当な語(句)を選びなさい。【表現と文法の知識】 (各 2 点)

   (2) ア. because   イ. how   ウ. where   エ. why

   (3) ア. is being destroyed   イ. is being determined

       ウ. is being planned   エ. is destroying

   (4) ア. Above all   イ. As a result

       ウ. At the same time   エ. For example

3. 下線部(5)は具体的には何を指していますか。日本語で答えなさい。
【内容についての思考力・判断力・表現力】(3 点)

4. 次の問いに英語で答えなさい。【内容についての思考力・判断力・表現力】 (各 4 点)

   (1) Where are the jungle schools for orangutans?

   (2) Why can't the orangutans at these schools live in the real wilderness?

A Translate the English into Japanese and the Japanese into English.【語彙の知識】（各1点）

1. _____ 名 B1　スローガン

2. unity 名　　　　　　　　[　　　　　　　]

3. foreign-born 形　　　[　　　　　　　]

4. _____ 動 B1　…を団結させる

5. _____ 形 B1　多様な, 異なった

6. diversity 名　　　　　[　　　　　　　]

B Choose the word whose underlined part is pronounced differently from the other three.【発音の知識】　　　　　　　　　　　　　　　（各2点）

1. ア. cr<u>ea</u>te　　　イ. d<u>a</u>nger　　　ウ. f<u>a</u>mous　　　エ. gr<u>a</u>dually

2. ア. f<u>o</u>llow　　　イ. pr<u>o</u>duct　　　ウ. sl<u>o</u>gan　　　エ. s<u>o</u>lve

3. ア. cr<u>i</u>ticize　　イ. pr<u>i</u>mitive　　ウ. un<u>i</u>te　　　エ. w<u>i</u>lderness

C Complete the following English sentences to match the Japanese.【表現と文法の知識】

（各3点）

1. 昨日は天気が悪かったが, 今日はさらに悪い。

The weather was bad yesterday, but it is (　　　　　　　) worse today.

2. 私はチームの一員であることを楽しみました。

I enjoyed being (　　　　　　) (　　　　　　) a team.

3. 四つ葉のクローバーは幸運の象徴とみなされている。

The four-leaf clover is seen (　　　　　　) a symbol of good luck.

D Arrange the words in the proper order to match the Japanese.【表現と文法の知識・技能】

（各3点）

1. チーズやバターは牛乳から作られる製品である。

Cheese and butter (are / from / made / milk / products).

_____

2. すみませんが, お借りできるペンをお持ちでしょうか。

Excuse me, do you (a pen / borrow / could / have / I)?

_____

3. そのオーケストラとの共演は, 彼が音楽家として成長するのに役立った。

Playing with the orchestra (a musician / as / grow / helped / him).

_____

E Read the following passage and answer the questions below.

"One Team" was Japan's slogan for the 2019 Rugby World Cup. Sixteen of Japan's 31 players were born in other nations. (1)The unity shown by these players of different backgrounds surely moved the public.

Captain Michael Leitch, a New Zealand-born Japanese, created various opportunities for the foreign-born players to learn about Japan. For example, (2)he held quiz events to teach them about the country's history. Michael said, "If they learn more about Japan, we can become even more united as one team."

The team can be seen (3) a mirror of (4)today's Japan. Many people from diverse backgrounds are gradually becoming part of Japanese society. (5), the diversity they bring can help Japan build a new era.

1. 下線部(1)の文の主語と(述語)動詞をそれぞれ一語で答えなさい。【文法の知識】　　（各1点）

主語：(　　　　　　　　)　　　　　　(述語) 動詞：(　　　　　　　　)

2. 下線部(2)の最終的な目的を，日本語で答えなさい。【内容についての思考力・判断力・表現力】　（3点）

3. 空所(3), (5)に入る最も適当な語（句）を選びなさい。【表現と文法の知識】　　（各2点）

(3) ア. as　　　　　イ. for　　　　　ウ. like　　　　　エ. to

(5) ア. As a result　　イ. However　　ウ. In addition to　　エ. In contrast

4. 下線部(4)の特徴はどのようなものですか。日本語で答えなさい。

【内容についての思考力・判断力・表現力】（3点）

5. 次の問いに英語で答えなさい。【内容についての思考力・判断力・表現力】　　（各4点）

(1) How many foreign-born players were there on the 2019 Japanese national rugby team?

(2) What does the team reflect?

/50

A Translate the English into Japanese and the Japanese into English.【語彙の知識】（各1点）

1. .... 名 B2 不死, 不滅　　2. factor 名 B2　　　[　　　　　]

3. .... 動　…を活性化する　4. longevity 名　　　[　　　　　]

5. intake 名　　　[　　　　　]　　6. .... 動 B1 回復する

B Choose the word whose underlined part is pronounced differently from the other three.【発音の知識】（各2点）

1. ア. argue　　イ. researcher　　ウ. turn　　エ. work

2. ア. agree　　イ. damage　　ウ. gene　　エ. longevity

3. ア. intake　　イ. life　　ウ. retire　　エ. unlikely

C Complete the following English sentences to match the Japanese.【表現と文法の知識】

（各3点）

1. これらの出来事が第二次世界大戦を引き起こした。

These events (　　　　　　　) to World War II.

2. 彼女に一緒に来てほしいが, 見込みは薄い。

I want her to come with me, but it's very (　　　　　　　).

3. 犬の平均寿命は10年から13年と言われている。

It is said that the average (　　　　　　) (　　　　　　) of a dog is 10 to 13 years.

D Arrange the words in the proper order to match the Japanese.【表現と文法の知識・技能】

（各3点）

1. 私にその書類を送ってもらうことはできますか。

(it / to / possible / is) send me those documents?

2. 母が新しい靴を選ぶのを手伝ってくれた。

(choose / helped / me / my mother) new shoes.

3. その機器を使うのをやめたほうがいいと主張する人もいた。

(argued / some / that / we) should stop using the device.

E Read the following passage and answer the questions below.

Everyone hopes to be healthy and live a long life. Will it ever (1)(be / for / humans / possible / to) gain immortality, then?

Researchers hold different views on this question. Some argue that everlasting life will be possible in the future, (2) others think it's unlikely. However, many of them seem to agree that we can delay aging. One of the key factors is to activate our "longevity genes." This could be made possible, for example, by reducing our calorie intake. The activated genes could help damaged cells recover. Moreover, they might also prevent some serious diseases.

(3)(extending / lead / may / our life span / to) great changes in our society. People might retire (4) the age of 85, or centenarian athletes might even take part (5) the Olympics!

1. 下線部(1), (3)の(　　)内の語句を適切に並べかえなさい。【表現の知識】　　　　　　(各3点)

   (1) _____

   (3) _____

2. 空所(2)に入る最も適当な語を選びなさい。【語彙と表現の知識】　　　　　　(2点)

   ア. because　　　　イ. if　　　　　　ウ. since　　　　エ. while

3. 空所(4), (5)に入る最も適当な語を選びなさい。【語彙と表現の知識】　　　　　(各2点)

   ア. at　　　　　　イ. for　　　　　　ウ. in　　　　　エ. on

   (4) (　　　　)　　(5) (　　　　　)

4. 次の問いに英語で答えなさい。【内容についての思考力・判断力・表現力】　　　　　(各4点)

   (1) How could we activate longevity genes?

   _____

   (2) Why is activating longevity genes one of the key factors for delaying aging?

   _____

/50

A Translate the English into Japanese and the Japanese into English. 【語彙の知識】(各1点)

1. ＿＿＿＿＿＿ 名 B2　トンネル
2. novel 名 A2　[　　　　]
3. ＿＿＿＿＿＿ 名 B1　学者
4. explicit 形　[　　　　]
5. objectively 副　[　　　]
6. ＿＿＿＿＿＿ 副　主観的に

B Choose the word which has primary stress on a different syllable from the other three. 【アクセントの知識】(各2点)

1. ア. dis-play　　　イ. nov-el　　　ウ. schol-ar　　　エ. tun-nel
2. ア. ad-di-tion　　イ. ex-plic-it　　ウ. scen-er-y　　エ. trans-la-tion
3. ア. lit-er-a-ture　イ. ob-jec-tive-ly　ウ. o-rig-i-nal　エ. sub-jec-tive-ly

C Complete the following English sentences to match the Japanese. 【表現と文法の知識】(各3点)

1. 彼はバイクを2台持っている。さらに，車を5台持っている。

He has two motorcycles. (　　　　) (　　　　), he has five cars.

2. 業績をできるだけ客観的に評価することが大切だ。

It is important to evaluate the performance as (　　　) as possible.

3. 彼は兄を観察して多くのことを学んでいる。

He learns a lot (　　　　) (　　　　) his brother.

D Arrange the words in the proper order to match the Japanese. 【表現と文法の知識・技能】(各3点)

1. この小説は日本の有名な作家によって翻訳された。

(by / this novel / translated / was) a famous Japanese writer.

＿＿＿＿＿＿＿＿＿＿＿＿＿＿＿＿＿＿＿＿＿＿＿＿＿＿＿＿

2. 物事には様々な見方がある。

There are (different / of / seeing / ways) things.

＿＿＿＿＿＿＿＿＿＿＿＿＿＿＿＿＿＿＿＿＿＿＿＿＿＿＿＿

3. テストの点数を他の人のものと比べてはいけません。

You should not (compare / those / with / your test scores) of others.

＿＿＿＿＿＿＿＿＿＿＿＿＿＿＿＿＿＿＿＿＿＿＿＿＿＿＿＿

E Read the following passage and answer the questions below.

The train came out of the long tunnel into the snow country.

This is the opening passage of the novel, *Snow Country*, (1)(write) by Yasunari Kawabata. This passage in English was translated by Edward George Seidensticker, an American scholar of Japanese literature. (2)(Compare) with the original, how is his translation different?

The sentence in the Japanese original has no explicit subject. (3), Seidensticker translated the sentence by using "the train" as the subject. (4) Japanese, subjects are usually required in English.

In addition, in the English version, the scenery is described objectively with a view from the sky, while it is viewed subjectively from inside the train in the Japanese original. In this way, (5)(compare / if / Japanese / novels / we / with) their English translations, we can observe their different ways of seeing the world.

1. 下線部(1), (2)の語を適切な形に変えなさい。【語彙の知識】　　　　（各2点）

   (1) ....

   (2) ....

2. 空所(3)に入る最も適当な語句を選びなさい。【語彙と表現の知識】　　　　（3点）

   ア. For example　　イ. In addition　　ウ. In short　　エ. On the other hand

3. 空所(4)に入る最も適当な語を選びなさい。【語彙の知識】　　　　（2点）

   ア. Alike　　　　イ. Like　　　　ウ. Likely　　　　エ. Unlike

4. 下線部(5)の(　　　)内の語を適切に並べかえなさい。【表現の知識】　　　　（3点）

5. 次の問いに英語で答えなさい。【内容についての思考力・判断力・表現力】　　　　（各4点）

   (1) What did Seidensticker use as the subject when he translated the opening passage of *Snow Country*?

   (2) How is the scenery in the opening passage of *Snow Country* described in the English version?

A Translate the English into Japanese and the Japanese into English.【語彙の知識】(各1点)

1. _____ 名 孤児院　　　　　2. miserable 形 B1　[　　　　　　　]

3. _____ 名 B2 起業家　　　　4. pursue 動 A2　[　　　　　　　]

5. distinguished 形 B2　[　　　　　　　]　6. _____ 形 B1 才能のある，有能な

B Choose the word which has primary stress on a different syllable from the other three.【アクセントの知識】　　　　　　　　　　　　　　　　　　　　　(各2点)

1. ア. a-ware　　　イ. in-vent　　　ウ. of-fer　　　エ. re-duce

2. ア. ath-lete　　イ. com-pose　　ウ. pur-sue　　エ. suc-cess

3. ア. ap-pli-ance　イ. dis-tin-guished　ウ. es-tab-lish　エ. tal-ent-ed

C Complete the following English sentences to match the Japanese.【表現と文法の知識】

(各3点)

1. 私はあなたが直面している問題に気づいていませんでした。

I was not (　　　　　　) (　　　　　　) the problems you faced.

2. 彼らは，貧しい子供たちのための学校を設立するためにお金を必要としていた。

They needed the money to set (　　　　　　) a school for poor children.

3. 私たちは，困っている家庭を助けるために寄付を募っています。

We collect donations to help families (　　　　　　) need.

D Arrange the words in the proper order to match the Japanese.【表現と文法の知識・技能】

(各3点)

1. 去年の冬，私は沖縄に行きましたが，思っていたほど暖かくはありませんでした。

Last winter I went to Okinawa, (as / it / warm / wasn't / where) as I had expected.

_____

2. バッタには強くて長い脚があり，そのおかげで高く跳ぶことができる。

A grasshopper has strong long legs that (able / it / jump / make / to) high.

_____

3. あなたの言うことがよくわからない。言いたいことの例を一つあげてくれないか。

I don't quite understand you. Can you give me (mean / of / one example / what / you)?

_____

E Read the following passage and answer the questions below.

Keisuke Honda is a well-known professional soccer player. In 2010, Keisuke was in South Africa to play in the World Cup. He visited an orphanage, where he saw many miserable children. (1)This experience made him aware of what he could do to (2) the world a better place.

Now, as an entrepreneur, Keisuke is trying hard to (3)(offer / opportunities / people / pursue / to) their dreams. (4), he established soccer schools inside and outside Japan. Next, he set up funds with famous and distinguished people all over the world. As a gifted and talented person, he is conscious (5) his mission to give people in need a path to success.

1. 下線部(1)の具体的な内容を，日本語で答えなさい。【内容についての思考力・判断力・表現力】　　（3点）

2. 空所(2), (4), (5)に入る最も適当な語(句)を選びなさい。【語彙と表現の知識】　　（各2点）
   (2) ア. become 　　　イ. give 　　　ウ. make 　　　エ. show
   (4) ア. At first 　　　　　　　イ. First of all
       ウ. For the first time 　　　エ. From the first
   (5) ア. for 　　　　　イ. of 　　　　　ウ. on 　　　　　エ. to

3. 下線部(3)の(　　　)内の語を適切に並べかえなさい。【表現の知識】　　（3点）

4. 次の問いに英語で答えなさい。【内容についての思考力・判断力・表現力】　　（各4点）
   (1) Who helped Keisuke set up funds?

   (2) What is his mission as a gifted and talented person?

Practice

/50

A Translate the English into Japanese and the Japanese into English. 【語彙の知識】(各1点)

1. .... 形 B1 仮想の　　　　　　2. heroine 名　　　[　　　　　　]

3. .... 動 A2 …を応用する　　　4. surgeon 名 B1　[　　　　　　]

5. complex 形 B1　[　　　　　]　　6. .... 名 B1 手術

B Choose the word which has primary stress on a different syllable from the other three. 【アクセントの知識】(各2点)

1. ア. con-tin-ue　　イ. her-o-ine　　ウ. med-i-cal　　エ. vir-tu-al

2. ア. Aus-tral-ia　　イ. ben-e-fit　　ウ. e-lec-tric　　エ. pro-duc-er

3. ア. ge-og-ra-phy　　イ. grad-u-al-ly　　ウ. lit-er-a-ture　　エ. mis-er-a-ble

C Complete the following English sentences to match the Japanese. 【表現と文法の知識】

(各3点)

1. 彼は服を脱いでパジャマを着ました。

He took off his clothes and (　　　　　　) (　　　　　　) pajamas.

2. A: パンとチーズと紅茶と砂糖を買うつもりです。　B: ミルクも買ってきてくれる？

A: I'm going to get bread, cheese, tea and sugar.

B: Can you get some milk as (　　　　　　)?

3. このままどんどん大きくなり続ければ，彼は本当にすごく背が高くなるわ。

If he (　　　　　) (　　　　　　) growing like that, he'll be really tall.

D Arrange the words in the proper order to match the Japanese. 【表現と文法の知識・技能】

(各3点)

1. 私の娘は前々からずっと医学の分野に興味を持っていました。

My daughter has always (been / in / interested / of / the field) medicine.

2. この技術は産業界のさまざまな問題を解決するのに応用することができる。

This technology can be (applied / in / problems / solving / to) industry.

3. コンピュータの技術がさらに普及しても，印刷された書籍は利用され続けるだろう。

Even if computer technology becomes more widespread, printed books (be / continue / to / used / will).

E Read the following passage and answer the questions below.

VR (virtual reality) technology has been developing in the field of entertainment. (1)The moment we put on head-mounted VR goggles, we can dive into a virtual world and become a hero or a heroine in a game.

(2) entertainment, VR technology has been applied to (3)other fields as well. First, this technology is also used in medical fields. It is used by surgeons to rehearse complex operations. Second, teachers can apply this technology to their classrooms. In a geography class, (4), students can visit any place on the globe on a virtual field trip. Third, VR-based training is offered to prepare against natural disasters.

VR technology will surely keep on developing. We can continue to expect many surprising benefits from it.

1. 下線部(1)とほぼ同じ意味になるように，（　　）に適語を補いなさい。【語彙と表現の知識】 （2点）

As (　　　　　　　　) as we put on head-mounted VR goggles,

2. 空所(2)，(4)に入る最も適当な語句を選びなさい。

【表現の知識，内容についての思考力・判断力・表現力】（各2点）

(2) ア. Due to　　　　イ. In addition to　ウ. In spite of　　エ. Instead of
(4) ア. as a result　　イ. first of all　　ウ. for example　　エ. in addition

3. 下線部(3)の具体的な分野を，日本語で答えなさい。【内容についての思考力・判断力・表現力】 （6点）

4. 次の問いに英語で答えなさい。【内容についての思考力・判断力・表現力】 （各4点）

(1) What can we do by wearing VR goggles?

(2) What can surgeons do with VR technology?

A Translate the English into Japanese and the Japanese into English.【語彙の知識】(各1点)

1. .... 名 A2 個性, 性格　　2. knowledge 名 A2　[　　　　　]

3. .... 動 B2 …に取りつく　4. ichthyology 名　[　　　　　]

5. prove 動 B1　[　　　　]　6. .... 形　准…, 準…

B Choose the word whose underlined part is pronounced differently from the other three.【発音の知識】(各2点)

1. ア. el<u>e</u>mentary　イ. <u>e</u>ven　　ウ. obs<u>e</u>ss　　エ. prof<u>e</u>ssor

2. ア. ar<u>ch</u>itect　イ. <u>ch</u>ildhood　ウ. i<u>ch</u>thyology　エ. s<u>ch</u>ool

3. ア. as<u>s</u>ociate　イ. pr<u>o</u>ve　　ウ. <u>sh</u>oulder　エ. <u>th</u>ough

C Complete the following English sentences to match the Japanese.【表現と文法の知識】

(各3点)

1. 彼はいつも自分の能力を示したがる。

He always wants to (　　　　　) (　　　　　).

2. 私は駅で伯父さんに会えなかった。

I (　　　　　) to meet my uncle at the station.

3. その子は母親の絵を描き, さらにその絵をきれいに塗った。

The child drew a picture of her mother, and (　　　　　), she then painted it beautifully.

D Arrange the words in the proper order to match the Japanese.【表現と文法の知識・技能】

(各3点)

1. 私は父の勤勉さを尊敬しています。

I (for / his diligence / my father / respect).

2. その先生は潔癖症だった。

The teacher (being / obsessed / was / with) clean.

3. そのカバンは軽いだけでなく, 機能的でもある。

The bag is (but / light / not / only) also functional.

E Read the following passage and answer the questions below.

With a boxfish on his head, Sakana-kun often appears on TV. He is popular for his cheerful personality. (1), he is respected for his knowledge of fish.

As a child, Sakana-kun liked fish. He also liked drawing. He was obsessed with (2)(draw) fish and didn't study at all. His elementary school teacher (3)(asked / him / his mother / make / to) study. But she answered, "He really likes fish, and I'm happy (4)(he / is / just / the way / with)."

His childhood dream was to become an ichthyology professor. Though he failed to enter university, he worked hard and proved himself in the ichthyology field. Later, he was (5)(invite) to join a university as a visiting associate professor. His consistent love for fish enabled him to realize his dream.

1. 空所(1)に入る最も適当な語を選びなさい。【語彙と表現の知識】　　　　　　(2 点)

　　ア. Consequently　　イ. First　　　　ウ. However　　エ. Moreover

2. 下線部(2), (5)の語を適切な形に変えなさい。【文法の知識】　　　　　　（各 2 点)

　　(2) ....

　　(5) ....

3. 下線部(3), (4)の(　　)内の語句を適切に並べかえなさい。【表現の知識】　　（各 3 点)

　　(3) ....

　　(4) ....

4. 次の問いに英語で答えなさい。【内容についての思考力・判断力・表現力】　　（各 4 点)

　　(1) What is Sakana-kun respected for?

　　..

　　(2) What enabled Sakana-kun to realize his dream?

　　..

Practice

/50

A Translate the English into Japanese and the Japanese into English. 【語彙の知識】 (各1点)

1. .... 動 B1 …に動機を与える　　2. transparent 形 B2 　　[　　　　　　]

3. .... 副 B1 きちんと，適切に　　4. separation 名 B1 　　[　　　　　　]

5. artifice 名　　[　　　　]　　6. .... 名 B1 費用，出費

B Choose the word which has primary stress on a different syllable from the other three. 【アクセントの知識】　　(各2点)

1. ア. ar-ti-fice　　イ. cor-rect-ly　　ウ. oth-er-wise　　エ. prop-er-ly

2. ア. dec-o-rate　　イ. mo-ti-vate　　ウ. sep-a-rate　　エ. trans-par-ent

3. ア. e-co-nom-ic　　イ. es-ca-la-tor　　ウ. mo-ti-va-tion　　エ. sep-a-ra-tion

C Complete the following English sentences to match the Japanese. 【表現と文法の知識】

(各3点)

1. 誤ってその女性の足を踏んでしまった。

I (　　　　　　) (　　　　　　　　) the woman's foot by accident.

2. ここに透明のプラスチックの箱をいくつか置きましょう。

Let's put some (　　　　　　) plastic boxes here.

3. 私はまだこの街のごみ分別ルールに慣れていない。

I'm not yet used to the (　　　　　) (　　　　　　) rules of this city.

D Arrange the words in the proper order to match the Japanese. 【表現と文法の知識・技能】

(各3点)

1. 子供を勉強する気にさせるのは難しくはない。

It is not difficult to (children / motivate / study / to).

2. 私にとってそれは悪い知らせというより，むしろ良い知らせであった。

For me, it was (bad news / good news / rather / than).

3. たくさんお金を持っている親は子供を甘やかしそうだとよく言われる。

It is often said that parents who have much money (are / likely / spoil / their children / to).

E Read the following passage and answer the questions below.

These are stairs (1)(decorate) like a piano. We can actually make a piano-like sound by stepping on the stairs. This motivates us to use the stairs rather than the escalator. (2)(is / not / only / the stairs / using) fun but also good for our health.

This transparent trash bin allows us to see the garbage inside it. We are more likely to separate garbage properly; (3) we may look bad to others around us. (4), we are more likely to follow the garbage separation rules after seeing the garbage already separated correctly.

Just small artifices like these evoke behavioral changes to solve personal or social problems. (5)They don't require high-tech devices or lots of expense, and they can change people's behaviors for the better.

1. 下線部(1)の語を適切な形に変えなさい。【表現と文法の知識】　　　　　　　　　　(2 点)

   ....

2. 下線部(2)の(　　)内の語句を適切に並べかえなさい。【表現の知識】　　　　　　　(3 点)

   ....

3. 空所(3), (4)に入る最も適当な語(句)を選びなさい。【語彙と表現の知識】　　　　　(各 2 点)

   (3) ア. besides　　　イ. however　　　ウ. moreover　　　エ. otherwise
   (4) ア. For example　イ. In addition　ウ. Nevertheless　エ. On the other hand

4. 下線部(5)が指すものを，本文中から抜き出しなさい。【内容についての思考力・判断力・表現力】(3 点)

   ....

5. 次の問いに英語で答えなさい。【内容についての思考力・判断力・表現力】　　　　(各 4 点)

   (1) What happens when people step on the stairs with piano decorations?

   ....

   (2) What are we likely to do after seeing the garbage already separated correctly?

   ....

Ⓐ Translate the English into Japanese and the Japanese into English. 【語彙の知識】 (各1点)

1. _____ 動 …を蘇らせる
2. inherit 動 B2 [   ]
3. _____ 形 B2 戦時の
4. colorization 名 [   ]
5. closeness 名 [   ]
6. _____ 動 じっと見つめる

Ⓑ Choose the word which has primary stress on a different syllable from the other three. 【アクセントの知識】   (各2点)

1. ア. in-her-it   イ. re-al-ize   ウ. sep-a-rate   エ. var-i-ous
2. ア. cal-o-rie   イ. col-or-ize   ウ. se-ri-ous   エ. sur-vi-vor
3. ア. cer-e-mo-ny イ. es-ca-la-tor ウ. ex-pe-ri-ence エ. or-di-nar-y

Ⓒ Complete the following English sentences to match the Japanese. 【表現と文法の知識】

(各3点)

1. 多くの人がその結婚式の計画に関わっていた。

   A lot of people were (   ) in planning the wedding.
2. ジェーンは10時に出て行き，そのすぐ後に私も出て行きました。

   Jane left at ten o'clock and I left (   ) (   ).
3. 糖分を摂りすぎると，あらゆる種類の健康問題を引き起こしかねない。

   Eating too much sugar can (   ) to all sorts of health problems.

Ⓓ Arrange the words in the proper order to match the Japanese. 【表現と文法の知識・技能】

(各3点)

1. かつては，人は2本の棒をこすり合わせて火をおこした。

   People used to (by / fire / make / rubbing / two sticks) together.

2. 入場の際，チケットをドアのところに立っている男性にお渡しください。

   When you enter, please hand your ticket (at / standing / the door / the man / to).

3. ブライアンの運転は最悪だ。まるで道路を走っているのは自分だけかのように車を走らせる。

   Brian is a terrible driver. He drives (as / he / if / the only driver / were) on the road.

E Read the following passage and answer the questions below.

　　Anju Niwata and Professor Hidenori Watanave have been involved in the "Rebooting Memories" project.　This project aims to inherit memories of war by colorizing prewar and wartime black-and-white photos.　These photos are colorized (1)based (　　) AI technology and conversations (　2　) war survivors.

　　In 2017, (3)as a high school student, Anju met a man who had experienced war and listened to his story.　Soon after, she learned about colorization technology in Watanave's workshop, and then colorized his photos.　Seeing the colorized photos, Anju and the man felt (4)(a sense / closeness / of / the past events / to) in the photos.

　　(5)These encounters led to their project.　They colorized photos of people's daily lives during wartime: a family under cherry blossoms and a couple gazing at a burnt-out city.　The people in these photos look alive, as if they were actually in front of us.

1. 下線部(1)が「…に基づいて」という意味になるように，(　　)に適語を補いなさい。

【語彙と表現の知識】（2点）

　　based (　　　　　　　　) …

2. 空所(2)に入る最も適当な語を選びなさい。【語彙と表現の知識】　　　　　　　（2点）

　　ア. about　　　　　イ. on　　　　　　ウ. to　　　　　　エ. with

3. 下線部(3)とほぼ同じ意味になるように，(　　)に適語を補いなさい。【語彙と表現の知識】　（2点）

　　(　　　　　　　　) she was a high school student

4. 下線部(4)の(　　)内の語句を適切に並べかえなさい。【表現の知識】　　　　　（3点）

5. 下線部(5)の具体的な内容を，日本語で答えなさい。【内容についての思考力・判断力・表現力の知識】（3点）

6. 次の問いに英語で答えなさい。【内容についての思考力・判断力・表現力】　　　　（各4点）

　　(1) What is the aim of the "Rebooting Memories" project?

　　(2) What photos did Anju and Watanave colorize?

A Translate the English into Japanese and the Japanese into English. 【語彙の知識】 (各1点)

1. _____ 副 B1　公式に，正式に　　2. smallpox 名　　　[　　　　　　]

3. _____ 名　　予防接種，ワクチン接種　4. treatment 名 B1　[　　　　　　]

5. devastating 形 B1　[　　　　　]　6. _____ 名　　根絶，撲滅

B Choose the word which has primary stress on a different syllable from the other three. 【アクセントの知識】　(各2点)

1. ア. ap-ply　　　イ. pre-pare　　　ウ. u-nit　　　エ. u-nite

2. ア. col-or-ize　　イ. con-trib-ute　　ウ. mo-ti-vate　　エ. vic-to-ry

3. ア. dev-as-tat-ing　イ. e-rad-i-cate　ウ. of-fi-cial-ly　エ. suc-cess-ful-ly

C Complete the following English sentences to match the Japanese. 【表現と文法の知識】

(各3点)

1. その川はまだ汚染が除去されていない。

The river is not yet (　　　　　　　) of pollution.

2. 何百万もの人々がロックンロールを愛している。

(　　　　　) (　　　　　　　　) people love rock and roll music.

3. チームのみんながゲームの勝利に貢献した。

Everyone on the team (　　　　　　) (　　　　　　　) winning the game.

D Arrange the words in the proper order to match the Japanese. 【表現と文法の知識・技能】

(各3点)

1. 試験に合格した生徒は彼らだけだった。

They were (passed / students / that / the exam / the only).

2. 弁護士や医師は依頼人や患者のプライバシーを守らなければならない。

Lawyers and doctors are required to protect (of / pay / the people / the privacy / who) for their services.

3. チケットなしにはどなたも美術館には入場できません。

No (enter / may / the museum / visitor / without) a ticket.

E Read the following passage and answer the questions below.

The WHO officially declared the world free of smallpox in 1980. This was the (1) of a WHO global vaccination campaign. Today, smallpox is the only infectious disease that humans have successfully eradicated. (2)(   ) effective treatment for smallpox exists, and this devastating disease killed millions of people in the past.

There was a Japanese physician who contributed to the global eradication of smallpox. He is Dr. Isao Arita. He headed the WHO Smallpox Eradication Unit from 1977 to 1985. He was awarded the Japan Prize in 1988 for (3)this great contribution. (4)The victory over smallpox is considered the most remarkable achievement in the history of international public health.

1. 空所(1)に入る最も適当な語を選びなさい。【語彙と表現の知識】 （3点）

　　ア. award 　　　　　イ. cause 　　　　　ウ. disease 　　　　　エ. result

2. 下線部(2)が「天然痘に対する効果的な治療法はない」という意味になるように，（　　）に適語を補いなさい。【表現と文法の知識】 （3点）

　　(　　　　　　　　　) effective treatment for smallpox exists

3. 下線部(3)の具体的な内容を，日本語で答えなさい。【内容についての思考力・判断力・表現力】 （3点）

_____

4. 下線部(4)とほぼ同じ意味で用いられている表現を，本文中から抜き出しなさい。

【内容についての思考力・判断力・表現力】（3点）

_____

5. 次の問いに英語で答えなさい。【内容についての思考力・判断力・表現力】 （各4点）

　　(1) What brought about the global eradication of smallpox?

_____

　　(2) To what did Dr. Isao Arita's work make a great contribution?

_____

A Translate the English into Japanese and the Japanese into English.【語彙の知識】(各1点)

1. ＿＿＿＿＿＿ 名　解毒，体内浄化　　2. refrain 動　[　　　　　]

3. ＿＿＿＿＿＿ 名 B1　関わり，交流　　4. distraction 名 B2　[　　　　　]

5. rewarding 形　[　　　　]　　6. ＿＿＿＿＿＿ 形　注意して，心を配って

B Choose the word whose underlined part is pronounced differently from the other three.【発音の知識】(各2点)

1. ア. digital　　　　イ. fatigue　　　ウ. inside　　　　エ. interaction

2. ア. detox　　　　イ. electronic　　ウ. follow　　　　エ. other

3. ア. artist　　　　イ. hard　　　　ウ. rewarding　　エ. smartphone

C Complete the following English sentences to match the Japanese.【表現と文法の知識】(各3点)

1. 祖父は今年の収穫に不安を感じている。

My grandfather feels (　　　　　　) about this year's harvest.

2. 子供たちはテレビに釘付けになってる。

The children (　　　　) (　　　　　) (　　　　　) the television.

3. 凍結した道路状況に気を配ったほうがいいよ。

You should be (　　　　　) (　　　　　　) the icy road conditions.

D Arrange the words in the proper order to match the Japanese.【表現と文法の知識・技能】(各3点)

1. あの看板に「ここでの喫煙は控えてください。」と書いてある。

That sign says "Please (from / here / refrain / smoking)."

2. その贈答品は賄賂としてはみなされなかった。

The gift (as / not / seen / was) a bribe.

3. 私は，疲労回復に役立つ栄養を摂取するようにしている。

I try to get the nutrition (help / me / recover / that / will) from fatigue.

E Read the following passage and answer the questions below.

Just walk down a busy street and look (1)(around / happening / see / to / what's). You will find that many people are glued to their smartphones. These people may need a digital detox.

A digital detox means to refrain from using electronic devices connected to the Internet, such as smartphones and computers. "Detoxing" from digital devices is often (2)(see) as a way to focus (3) real-life social interactions without distractions.

You might feel anxious, bored, and even annoyed without your smartphone and other tech tools. However, a digital detox can be a rewarding experience that will help to rest your (4)(exhaust) brain, relieve social media fatigue, and improve the quality of sleep. (5)(don't / down / put / why / you) your digital devices sometimes and be mindful of your other activities and experiences?

1. 下線部(1), (5)の(　　)内の語を適切に並べかえなさい。【表現の知識】　　　　(各3点)

　　(1) _____

　　(5) _____

2. 下線部(2), (4)の語を適切な形に変えなさい。【語彙の知識】　　　　(各2点)

　　(2) _____

　　(4) _____

3. 空所(3)に入る最も適当な語を選びなさい。【語彙の知識】　　　　(2点)

　　ア. as　　　　　　イ. in　　　　　　ウ. on　　　　　　エ. to

4. 次の問いに英語で答えなさい。【内容についての思考力・判断力・表現力】　　　　(各4点)

　　(1) What is a digital detox?

　　_____

　　(2) Who needs a digital detox?

　　_____

Practice

/50

A Translate the English into Japanese and the Japanese into English.【語彙の知識】(各1点)

1. _____ 名　足跡, フットプリント　2. indicator 名　[　　　　　　　]

3. _____ 動 B1　…を計算する　　　4. instance 名 B1　[　　　　　　　]

5. aspect 名 B1　[　　　　　　　]　　6. _____ 動　…を視覚化する

B Choose the word which has primary stress on a different syllable from the other three.【アクセントの知識】　(各2点)

1. ア. as-pect　　　イ. fa-tigue　　　ウ. foot-print　　　エ. li-ter

2. ア. cal-cu-late　　イ. dis-trac-tion　　ウ. kil-o-gram　　エ. lim-it-ed

3. ア. e-lec-tron-ic　イ. in-di-ca-tor　　ウ. in-ter-ac-tion　エ. vac-ci-na-tion

C Complete the following English sentences to match the Japanese.【表現と文法の知識】

(各3点)

1. この地図アプリは距離を正確に測定することができる。

This map app can (　　　　　　) distances accurately.

2. 私はズボンを2着買った。

I bought (　　　　) (　　　　　) (　　　　　) trousers.

3. 同じ学校に通っているが, 私は彼女と一度も話をしたことがない。

I have never talked to her (　　　　) (　　　　　) we are in the same school.

D Arrange the words in the proper order to match the Japanese.【表現と文法の知識・技能】

(各3点)

1. 家賃は私の給料の約3分の1に等しい。

The rent (about / equal / is / to) one-third of my salary.

_____

2. 卵1パックが300円もするなんて思いもよらなかった。

I never expected that a carton of eggs would (300 yen / as / as / cost / much).

_____

3. この地域で大金を持ち歩くのは危険だ。

It is dangerous to carry (a / amount / large / money / of) with you in this area.

_____

E Read the following passage and answer the questions below.

A surprising amount of water is used in our daily lives. The term "water footprint" can be a good indicator of this. It refers to the amount of water that is used and (1)(pollute) in order to produce the goods or services we use. A water footprint can be calculated for any product.

(2), a cup of coffee needs 132 liters of water, and one margherita pizza requires 1,259 liters. The water footprint of one kilogram of beef is (3)(as / as / equal / much / to) 15,415 liters. A pair of jeans requires about 8,000 liters, and one car requires 52,000 - 83,000 liters!

It is important to realize that even though water is a (4)(limit) resource, we depend on it so much in every aspect of our lives. (5)(helps / the water footprint / this fact / visualize).

1. 下線部(1)，(4)の語を適切な形に変えなさい。【語彙の知識】 　　　　　　　　　(各2点)

(1) _____

(4) _____

2. 空所(2)に入る最も適当な語(句)を選びなさい。【語彙と表現の知識】 　　　　　　　(2点)

ア. For instance　　イ. However　　　ウ. In addition　　エ. In short

3. 下線部(3)，(5)の(　　)内の語句を適切に並べかえなさい。【表現の知識】 　　　　(各3点)

(3) _____

(5) _____

4. 次の問いに英語で答えなさい。【内容についての思考力・判断力・表現力】 　　　　(各4点)

(1) What is a "water footprint"?

_____

(2) How much is the water footprint of a pair of jeans?

_____

A Translate the English into Japanese and the Japanese into English. 【語彙の知識】(各1点)

1. _____ 形 B2 捨てられた　　　　2. orbit 動　　　　　[　　　　　　]

3. _____ 名 B1 電気通信　　　　　4. remotely 副　　　　[　　　　　　]

5. removal 名　　　　[　　　　　]　　6. _____ 名 B2 協力

B Choose the word which has primary stress on a different syllable from the other three. 【アクセントの知識】(各2点)

1. ア. cap-ture　　　　イ. con-trol　　　　ウ. count-less　　　　エ. or-bit

2. ア. con-se-quence　イ. ef-fec-tive　　　ウ. in-fec-tious　　　エ. re-mote-ly

3. ア. es-ti-mate　　　イ. re-mov-al　　　ウ. sat-el-lite　　　　エ. ve-hi-cle

C Complete the following English sentences to match the Japanese. 【表現と文法の知識】

(各3点)

1. ケーキをもう一切れいかがですか。

   Would you like another (　　　　　　) (　　　　　　) cake?

2. 卵は料理の仕方がたくさんある。

   There are many (　　　　　) (　　　　　) cook eggs.

3. ジョンはまだ仕事を終えていません。

   John hasn't finished his work (　　　　　).

D Arrange the words in the proper order to match the Japanese. 【表現と文法の知識・技能】

(各3点)

1. その街道は4世紀に作られたと言われている。

   It is (built / said / that / the road / was) in the 4th century.

   _____

2. 大勢の人々がその映画スターが出てくるのを待っていた。

   There were (a lot / for / of / people / waiting) the film star to come out.

   _____

3. 救命艇は，海上で人々の命を救うのに使われる船である。

   A lifeboat is (a boat / people's lives / save / to / used) at sea.

   _____

E Read the following passage and answer the questions below.

The Earth is surrounded by countless pieces of waste called "space debris." They are parts of abandoned rocket bodies and satellites. (1)(　　) is estimated (　　) there are more than 100 million pieces of space debris orbiting around the Earth.

Space debris travels (2) about eight kilometers per second. If it hits and damages satellites used for climate research, telecommunications and navigation, (3)it will lead to serious consequences.

Researchers have been studying ways to remove space debris. For example, they have developed a remotely controlled vehicle and a space net satellite designed to capture debris. (4), debris removal technology has not yet been (5) into practical use. Further international cooperation will be necessary for sustainable space development.

1. 下線部(1)が「…だと推定されている」という意味になるように, (　　)に適語を補いなさい。
【語彙と表現の知識】（2点）

（　　　　　　） is estimated （　　　　　　）…

2. 空所(2), (4), (5)に入る最も適当な語を選びなさい。【語彙と表現の知識】　　　　（各2点）

(2) ア. at 　　　　イ. for 　　　　ウ. in 　　　　エ. to

(4) ア. Besides 　　イ. Consequently 　ウ. However 　エ. Instead

(5) ア. called 　　イ. found 　　　ウ. made 　　　エ. put

3. 下線部(3)は何を指していますか。日本語で答えなさい。
【内容についての思考力・判断力・表現力】（4点）

....

4. 次の問いに英語で答えなさい。【内容についての思考力・判断力・表現力】　　　（各4点）

(1) How fast does space debris travel?

....

(2) What will we need for sustainable space development?

....

A Translate the English into Japanese and the Japanese into English. 【語彙の知識】(各1点)

1. ＿＿＿＿＿＿＿ 圖 B1　絶え間なく，連続的に　2. precipitation 图　[　　　　　　　]

3. ＿＿＿＿＿＿＿ 形 B1　異常な　　　　　4. downpour 图　[　　　　　　　]

5. rainfall 图 B1　[　　　　　　]　6. ＿＿＿＿＿＿＿ 图 B1　頻度

B Choose the word whose underlined part is pronounced differently from the other three. 【発音の知識】(各2点)

1. ア. al<u>i</u>ve　　イ. appl<u>i</u>ance　　ウ. cl<u>i</u>mate　　エ. cont<u>i</u>nuously

2. ア. fr<u>e</u>quent　　イ. h<u>e</u>roine　　ウ. spr<u>ea</u>d　　エ. tr<u>ea</u>sure

3. ア. fr<u>e</u>quency　　イ. ill<u>e</u>gal　　ウ. m<u>e</u>dia　　エ. pr<u>e</u>cipitation

C Complete the following English sentences to match the Japanese. 【表現と文法の知識】

(各3点)

1. トムはジムの家庭は裕福だと思っているが，実際はそうではない。

　Tom thinks Jim's family is rich, but in (　　　　　　　) they're not.

2. 車はとても役に立つが，ところが他方では，多大な環境汚染をもたらす。

　Cars are very useful, but (　　　　　　) the other (　　　　　　), they cause
　a huge amount of pollution.

3. チョコレートのような甘い食べ物は肥満の原因となりうる。

　Sweet foods such (　　　　　　) chocolate can make you fat.

D Arrange the words in the proper order to match the Japanese. 【表現と文法の知識・技能】

(各3点)

1. 今日はたぶん雨は降らないだろう。

　(is / it / it / that / unlikely) will rain today.

　＿＿＿＿＿＿＿＿＿＿＿＿＿＿＿＿＿＿＿＿＿＿＿＿＿＿＿＿＿＿＿

2. 彼が突然意見を変えたのはどういうわけだろう。

　What is (behind / his sudden change / of / opinion / the reason)?

　＿＿＿＿＿＿＿＿＿＿＿＿＿＿＿＿＿＿＿＿＿＿＿＿＿＿＿＿＿＿＿

3. コンピュータゲームは近頃ますます刺激的なものになっている。

　Computer games are (and / exciting / getting / more / more) these days.

　＿＿＿＿＿＿＿＿＿＿＿＿＿＿＿＿＿＿＿＿＿＿＿＿＿＿＿＿＿＿＿

E Read the following passage and answer the questions below.

In the animated movie, *Tenkinoko* (*Weathering with You*), it continues to rain for over two years, and as a result the city of Tokyo is changed a lot. Could (1)this actually happen in real life?

(2)It's unlikely that it would rain continuously for so long. In fact, the annual precipitation of Tokyo has barely changed at all over the last thirty years. On the other hand, however, it is a fact that abnormal weather such as heavy downpours is becoming more frequent in Japan. There have been increasing cases of heavy rainfall causing serious damage.

(3)(behind / of / one / such abnormal weather / the factors) is global warming. If we can't stop global warming, the frequency of heavy downpours may increase more and more. Now we must (4)(against / fight / more steps / take / to) global warming and to protect the Earth.

1. 下線部(1)は何を指していますか。日本語で答えなさい。

【内容についての思考力・判断力・表現力】（3 点）

2. 下線部(2)の根拠となる事実を，日本語で答えなさい。【内容についての思考力・判断力・表現力】（3 点）

3. 下線部(3)，(4)の（　　　）内の語句を適切に並べかえなさい。【表現と文法の知識】　　　（各3点）

　　(3)

　　(4)

4. 次の問いに英語で答えなさい。【内容についての思考力・判断力・表現力】　　　（各4点）

　　(1) What has not changed much for many years?

　　(2) What cases have been increasing?

No Rain, No Rainbow

 Part 1

/50

A Translate the English into Japanese and the Japanese into English.【語彙の知識】(各1点)

1. _____ 動　衝突する, ぶつかる　　2. surgery 名 B1　[　　　　　　]

3. confine 動 B2　[　　　　　　]　　4. _____ 名　リハビリテーション

5. _____ 名 B2　助言者, 師匠　　6. accomplish 動 B1　[　　　　　　]

B Choose the word which has primary stress on a different syllable from the other three.【アクセントの知識】(各2点)

1. ア. col-lide　　　イ. com-plete　　　ウ. con-fine　　　エ. men-tor

2. ア. ac-ci-dent　イ. phys-i-cal　　　ウ. sur-ger-y　　　エ. un-der-go

3. ア. ac-com-plish　イ. con-fi-dence　ウ. fi-nal-ly　　　エ. rec-og-nize

C Complete the following English sentences to match the Japanese.【表現と文法の知識】

(各3点)

1. 大きな彗星が地球に衝突したとしたら, 何が起こるだろうか。

What would happen if a large comet (　　　　　) (　　　　　) the Earth?

2. その女の子は一人で買い物に行くことができた。

The girl could go shopping (　　　　　) (　　　　　).

3. 私は空港で自分の便を逃し, そこで一晩を過ごさなくてはならなかった。

I missed my flight at the airport, (　　　　　) I had to stay overnight.

D Arrange the words in the proper order to match the Japanese.【表現と文法の知識・技能】

(各3点)

1. 彼はその村では「先生」と呼ばれていた。

He (as / referred / to / was) "sensei" in the village.

_____

2. 私はインフルエンザにかかり, 2日間寝たきりだった。

I got the flu and (bed / confined / to / was) for two days.

_____

3. このボタンを押しさえすればいいのです。

(all / do / need / to / you) is push this button.

_____

E Read the following passage and answer the questions below.

1 The accident happened in 2006, when I was 18. On my way home, my motorcycle collided with a car. After a 12-hour-long surgery, I barely survived. However, I (1)(I / that / told / was / would) spend the rest of my life confined to bed.

2 (2) six months of physical rehabilitation, I had learned to do many things by myself in a wheelchair. Then, I moved to another rehabilitation center, (3) I met my mentor in life. He was undergoing rehabilitation in the center, too. He always said to me, "Opportunity is under your feet. All you need to do is recognize it." He gave me several missions to accomplish, (4) going back home alone on the train. (5)(completing / given / had / he / the missions) me, I gradually gained confidence in myself. Finally, leaving the rehabilitation center in 2009, I decided to live alone.

1. 下線部(1), (5)の(　　)内の語句を適切に並べかえなさい。【表現と文法の知識】　　　　(各3点)

(1) ....

(5) ....

2. 空所(2), (3), (4)に入る最も適当な語を選びなさい。【表現と文法の知識】　　　　(各2点)

(2) ア. After　　　　イ. Before　　　　ウ. During　　　　エ. For

(3) ア. what　　　　イ. where　　　　ウ. which　　　　エ. why

(4) ア. for　　　　イ. like　　　　ウ. such　　　　エ. to

3. 次の問いに英語で答えなさい。【内容についての思考力・判断力・表現力】　　　　(各4点)

(1) How long did Tatsuya's surgery take?

....

(2) When did Tatsuya leave the rehabilitation center?

....

No Rain, No Rainbow

A Translate the English into Japanese and the Japanese into English.【語彙の知識】（各1点）

1. ＿＿＿＿＿＿ 名 A2 旅行，旅
2. fortunate 形 B1　[　　　　　　]
3. ＿＿＿＿＿＿ 名 B2 歩道
4. struggle 動 B2　[　　　　　　]
5. barrier 名 B2　[　　　　　]
6. ＿＿＿＿＿＿ 名 B1 優しさ，親切心

B Choose the word whose underlined part is pronounced differently from the other three.【発音の知識】(各2点)

1. ア. conf<u>i</u>ne　　イ. co<u>ll</u>ide　　ウ. f<u>i</u>x　　エ. k<u>i</u>ndness
2. ア. b<u>a</u>rrier　　イ. d<u>a</u>ngerous　　ウ. p<u>a</u>vement　　エ. v<u>a</u>cation
3. ア. f<u>or</u>tunate　　イ. j<u>our</u>ney　　ウ. s<u>ur</u>gery　　エ. w<u>or</u>ld

C Complete the following English sentences to match the Japanese.【表現と文法の知識】

(各3点)

1. あなたのご親切に感謝いたします。

Thank you for your (　　　　　　).

2. 私は今朝からずっとこの数学の問題を解こうと頑張っている。

I have been (　　　　　) (　　　　　) solve this math problem since this morning.

3. 彼は言語の壁を乗り越えるために一生懸命勉強した。

He worked hard to overcome the language (　　　　　).

D Arrange the words in the proper order to match the Japanese.【表現と文法の知識・技能】

(各3点)

1. 彼女は昨日そこにいなかったと私に言ったが，それは嘘だとわかった。

She told me she wasn't there yesterday, (be / out / to / turned / which) a lie.

2. 通りは人でごった返していた。

The street (full / of / people / was).

3. このケーキはなんて大きいの！

How (cake / huge / is / this)!

E Read the following passage and answer the questions below.

❸ In 2011, I traveled to Hawaii alone. It seemed like an enormous challenge, but my friends gave me a push. I enjoyed Hawaii to the fullest, (1) led to my next challenge: a journey around the world.

❹ I left Japan in 2017 and had fortunate encounters during the journey. Once, my wheelchair got (2)(break) on a stone pavement in Florence, Italy. Then, (3)(an Italian family / me / nearby / offered / passing) help and struggled to fix it for me. (4) lucky I was!

❺ I visited 23 countries in nine months. Through the journey, I found the world was still full of physical barriers. At the same time, I found these barriers could be overcome with the kindness of others. The motorcycle accident was a "rain" in my life, (5)(but / rain / thanks / that / to), I encountered many "rainbows" — wonderful people in the world.

1. 空所(1), (4)に入る最も適当な語を選びなさい。【表現の知識】　　　　　　　　(各2点)

   (1) ア. it　　　　　イ. that　　　　　ウ. where　　　　エ. which

   (4) ア. How　　　イ. What　　　　ウ. Who　　　　エ. Why

2. 下線部(2)の語を適切な形に変えなさい。【文法の知識】　　　　　　　　　　(2 点)

   ....

3. 下線部(3), (5)の(　　)内の語句を適切に並べかえなさい。【表現と文法の知識】　(各3点)

   (3) ....

   (5) ....

4. 次の問いに英語で答えなさい。【内容についての思考力・判断力・表現力】　　(各4点)

   (1) Did Tatsuya Miyo go to Hawaii with anyone else?

   ....

   (2) What does Tatsuya mean by many "rainbows"?

   ....

A Translate the English into Japanese and the Japanese into English.【語彙の知識】(各1点)

1. fascinated 形 B2　　　[　　　　　　　]　　2. priority 名 B2　　　　[　　　　　　　]

3. ＿＿＿＿＿ 形 B2 普遍的な, 万人共通の　4. accessible 形 B1　　　[　　　　　　　]

5. ＿＿＿＿＿ 副 B2 気にかけない　　　　　6. ＿＿＿＿＿ 名 B1 身体障害

B Choose the word which has primary stress on a different syllable from the other three.【アクセントの知識】 (各2点)

1. ア. anx-ious　　　イ. chal-lenge　　ウ. re-port　　　　エ. wheel-chair

2. ア. fas-ci-nat-ed　イ. in-ter-view-er　ウ. u-ni-ver-sal　エ. veg-e-ta-ble

3. ア. ac-ces-si-ble　　　　　　　　イ. en-cour-age-ment

　　ウ. grad-u-al-ly　　　　　　　　エ. pri-or-i-ty

C Complete the following English sentences to match the Japanese.【表現と文法の知識】

(各3点)

1. この建物は障害のある人にとって利用しやすいものではない。

This building is not accessible to people with (　　　　　　　).

2. 2～3日のんびりリラックスしたい。

I want to take (　　　　　　) (　　　　　　　) and relax for a few days.

3. 一歩踏み出してみませんか。

Why don't you take a (　　　　　　) (　　　　　　　)?

D Arrange the words in the proper order to match the Japanese.【表現と文法の知識・技能】

(各3点)

1. 私はその物語にすぐに引きつけられた。

I (by / fascinated / the story / was soon).

2. 政府は失業率を減らすことに重点を置くと約束した。

The government promised to (give / priority / reducing / to) unemployment.

3. 彼らは私たちの反対にもかかわらず，その計画を進めた。

They went forward with the plan (of / opposition / our / regardless).

E Read the following passage and answer the questions below.

Interviewer: I've (1)(hear) you're starting a new life in Okinawa. Could you tell me why?

Tatsuya: First of all, I love Okinawa. I'm fascinated by the amazing nature and the kindness of the people there. Also, Okinawa gives high priority to universal tourism, which is accessible to all people regardless of age, nationality and disability. There are things I want to report on (2) a wheelchair traveler.

Interviewer: I see. I'm looking forward to (3)(read) your report soon.

Tatsuya: Thank you.

Interviewer: You've challenged yourself in many things in your life so far. What would you like to say to (4)(are / hesitating / those / to / who) take a step forward like you?

Tatsuya: Well, I understand you'll feel anxious when you start something new. Just take it easy. (5)(are / around / people / watching / you) your efforts. They're ready to help you.

1. 下線部(1), (3)の語を適切な形に変えなさい。【表現と文法の知識】 　　　　(各2点)

　　(1) ....

　　(3) ....

2. 空所(2)に入る最も適当な語を選びなさい。【語彙の知識】 　　　　　　　(2点)

　　ア. as 　　　　　　　イ. for 　　　　　　　ウ. like 　　　　　　　エ. to

3. 下線部(4), (5)の(　　)内の語を適切に並べかえなさい。【表現と文法の知識】 　　(各3点)

　　(4) ....

　　(5) ....

4. 次の問いに英語で答えなさい。【内容についての思考力・判断力・表現力】 　　(各4点)

　　(1) In Okinawa, what fascinated Tatsuya?

　　..

　　(2) What kind of tourism does Okinawa give priority to?

　　..

Natto Saves People in Need Part 1

/50

A Translate the English into Japanese and the Japanese into English.【語彙の知識】(各1点)

1. powder 名 B1 [   ]　2. _____ 動 B1　…をかき混ぜる

3. _____ 動　…をろ過する　4. _____ 形 B2　濁った

5. sticky 形 B1 [   ]　6. purify 動 B1 [   ]

B Choose the word which has primary stress on a different syllable from the other three.【アクセントの知識】　(各2点)

1. ア. fil-ter　　　イ. pow-der　　　ウ. prod-uct　　　エ. suc-ceed

2. ア. at-ti-tude　イ. bar-ri-er　　ウ. com-po-nent　エ. pu-ri-fy

3. ア. e-lec-tron-ic　イ. ex-per-i-ment　ウ. in-flu-en-tial　エ. u-ni-ver-sal

C Complete the following English sentences to match the Japanese.【表現と文法の知識】

(各3点)

1. スプーン 2 杯の砂糖を加えなさい。

　　Add two (　　　　　　　) (　　　　　　　　　) sugar.

2. 最もよく使う道具はすぐ近くに置いておきなさい。

　　Keep the tools that you use most often close (　　　　　　　) (　　　　　　　).

3. 6 時間の登山の末，私たちは山頂にたどり着くことに成功した。

　　After six hours of climbing, we (　　　　　　　) (　　　　　　　) getting to the

　　top of the mountain.

D Arrange the words in the proper order to match the Japanese.【表現と文法の知識・技能】

(各3点)

1. その子は寂しいのです。遊び友達がいればもっと楽しいのですが。

　　The child is lonely; he would be happier if he (had / play / someone / to / with).

　　_____

2. 雨が降っているのが残念です。天気なら，海辺に散歩へ行くのですが。

　　It's a pity that it's raining now.　If it were fine, I (a walk / for / go / on / would) the beach.

　　_____

3. その数学の問題を解こうと一時間がんばって，彼はあきらめて助けを求めました。

　　After spending (an hour / solve / the math problem / to / trying), he gave up and asked for help.

　　_____

E Read the following passage and answer the questions below.

1 In a village in Bangladesh, a man (1) a spoonful of white powder into a beaker of dirty water taken from a local pond. He (2) it and the water becomes clear in a few minutes. He then (3) the water and (4) it. People say, "That powder is magic!"

2 The man's name is Kanetoshi Oda. In 1995, he experienced the Great Hanshin-Awaji Earthquake. At the time of that disaster, tap water was cut off and many people (5)were (   ) trouble. He thought, "How helpful it would be if we could use muddy pond water for drinking."

3 The (6) was unexpectedly close at hand. He remembered that the sticky component in *natto* — polyglutamic acid — can purify water. He spent years experimenting in his lab and finally succeeded in developing water purifying powder from polyglutamic acid.

1. 空所(1)〜(4)に入る最も適当な語をそれぞれ選びなさい。

【内容についての思考力・判断力・表現力】（各2点）

ア. drinks　　　イ. filters　　　ウ. puts　　　エ. stirs

(1) (　　　　)　　(2) (　　　　)　　(3) (　　　　)　　(4) (　　　　)

2. 下線部(5)が「困っていた」という意味になるように，(   )に適語を補いなさい。

【表現の知識】（2点）

were (　　　　　) trouble

3. 空所(6)に入る最も適当な語を選びなさい。【語彙の知識】　　　　　　　　（2点）

ア. difficulty　　　イ. problem　　　ウ. solution　　　エ. victory

4. 次の問いに英語で答えなさい。【内容についての思考力・判断力・表現力】　　　　（各4点）

(1) Why did Oda think about using pond water for drinking when he experienced the Great Hanshin-Awaji Earthquake?

(2) In what can we find polyglutamic acid?

A Translate the English into Japanese and the Japanese into English.【語彙の知識】（各1点）

1. purifier 名 [   ]   2. adopt 動 B1 [   ]

3. ＿＿＿＿＿＿ 形 B2 不十分な   4. effectively 副 B2 [   ]

5. ＿＿＿＿＿＿ 名 B1 雇用, 仕事   6. ＿＿＿＿＿＿ 形 B2 飲料に適した, 飲める

B Choose the word which has primary stress on a different syllable from the other three.【アクセントの知識】　　　　　　　　　　　　　　　　　　（各2点）

1. ア. a-dopt　　　イ. earth-quake　　ウ. ef-fort　　　　エ. mud-dy

2. ア. at-ten-tion　　イ. drink-a-ble　　ウ. qual-i-ty　　エ. rec-og-nize

3. ア. ef-fec-tive-ly　イ. pri-or-i-ty　　ウ. sub-se-quent-ly　エ. sus-tain-a-ble

C Complete the following English sentences to match the Japanese.【表現と文法の知識】

（各3点）

1. 彼はお金を節約するためにもっと小さなアパートに引っ越した。

He moved to a smaller apartment in (   ) to save money.

2. 彼女は走り高跳びと100メートル走の両方で記録を破った。

She broke the records in (   ) the high jump and the 100-meter sprint.

3. 私は勘定書をもらうためにウエイターの注意を引こうとした。

I tried to attract the waiter's (   ) so that I could get the bill.

D Arrange the words in the proper order to match the Japanese.【表現と文法の知識・技能】（各3点）

1. 社内の公用語として英語を用いるという新しい方針を採用している会社もある。

Some companies have (a new policy / adopted / English / of / using) as their official in-house language.

＿＿＿＿＿＿＿＿＿＿＿＿＿＿＿＿＿＿＿＿＿＿＿＿＿＿＿＿＿＿＿＿＿＿

2. 彼女はどうすればなれるのか知らないのに, 映画スターになりたいと夢見ていた。

She dreamed of becoming a movie star, even though she didn't (how / it / know / realize / to).

＿＿＿＿＿＿＿＿＿＿＿＿＿＿＿＿＿＿＿＿＿＿＿＿＿＿＿＿＿＿＿＿＿＿

3. ニューヨーク市は, 世界中からやってきた人々が共生する人種のるつぼと呼ばれている。

New York City is called (a melting pot / all over the world / from / people / where) live together.

＿＿＿＿＿＿＿＿＿＿＿＿＿＿＿＿＿＿＿＿＿＿＿＿＿＿＿＿＿＿＿＿＿＿

E Read the following passage and answer the questions below.

4 Unfortunately, Oda's water purifier didn't sell well in Japan. However, in 2004, when the Sumatra-Andaman Earthquake occurred, it was adopted to help victims in Thailand. (1)<u>This</u> attracted global attention and it was subsequently used in other countries such as Mexico, Bangladesh and Somalia.

5 Oda thought (2)(his product / insufficient / just / selling / was), however. So, he taught the local people how to effectively market it in order to create sustainable businesses. (3)<u>This</u> has given them both a steady supply of water and new employment. It has also improved their quality of life.

6 Oda's water purifier is now sold in over 40 countries and provides safe drinkable water to about 2.8 million people. He says, "Now I know (4)(born / for / I / was / what). While I am alive, I wish to create a world where everyone can get safe water."

1. 下線部(1), (3)は何を指していますか。日本語で答えなさい。

【内容についての思考力・判断力・表現力】（各3点）

　(1) ....

　(3) ....

2. 下線部(2), (4)の(　　)内の語(句)を適切に並べかえなさい。【表現と文法の知識】　　（各3点）

　(2) ....

　(4) ....

3. 次の問いに英語で答えなさい。【内容についての思考力・判断力・表現力】　　　（各4点）

　(1) What did Oda do in order to create sustainable businesses?

　...

　(2) What is his mission in life?

　...

Natto Saves People in Need

A Translate the English into Japanese and the Japanese into English.【語彙の知識】(各1点)

1. equipment 名 B1　　　[　　　　　　]　2. perspective 名 B2　　　[　　　　　　　]

3. _____ 動 B1　異なる　　　　　4. _____ 副 B2　緊急に

5. secure 動　　　　[　　　　　　]　6. _____ 動　…を理解する, …を把握する

B Choose the word which has primary stress on a different syllable from the other three.【アクセントの知識】

(各2点)

1. ア. ath-lete　　イ. man-age　　ウ. of-fer　　エ. se-cure

2. ア. ca-reer　　イ. com-plete　　ウ. dif-fer　　エ. sup-ply

3. ア. ad-van-tage　イ. con-trib-ute　ウ. per-spec-tive　エ. ur-gent-ly

C Complete the following English sentences to match the Japanese.【表現と文法の知識】

(各3点)

1. ハンバーガーを2つ食べましたが, 私はまだおなかがすいています。

I've eaten two hamburgers but I'm (　　　　　　) hungry.

2. バッグをテーブルの上に置いたままにしてはだめ。でないと盗まれるよ。

Don't leave your bag on the table, or it will get (　　　　　　).

3. ボディーランゲージは国によって違う。

Body language differs (　　　　　) country (　　　　　) country.

D Arrange the words in the proper order to match the Japanese.【表現と文法の知識・技能】

(各3点)

1. 人が石で道具を作れるようになった時代は, 石器時代と呼ばれる。

The period (humans / in / learned / to / which) make tools from stone is called the Stone Age.

_____

2. 彼は私に金を払ったと言っている。ところが, 私は彼から金を受け取っていない。

He says that he paid me, (have / I / not / received / while) any money from him.

_____

3. 海は世界を隔てているというよりむしろ結び付けている。

Oceans (divide / rather / than / the world / unite) it.

_____

E Read the following passage and answer the questions below.

In developing countries, there are still many people who cannot get safe drinking water. Building water wells might be one way to help these people. However, there are some points (1)(be / considered / need / that / to).

1. Just building water wells is not enough.

Water wells sometimes stop (2) when the equipment gets broken. In some cases, equipment parts are (3)(be / for / sold / stolen / to) profit. It is important to find ways in which local people can use and manage the wells sustainably. We need to have a long-term perspective.

2. Situations differ from place to place.

Some places urgently need wells to secure water, while (4) need developed water supply systems rather than wells. We have to grasp the actual situations and provide adequate support that (5) the needs of each case.

1. 下線部(1), (3)の(　　　)内の語を適切に並べかえなさい。【表現と文法の知識】　　(各3点)

(1) _____

(3) _____

2. 空所(2), (4), (5)に入る最も適当な語(句)を選びなさい。【語彙と表現の知識】　　(各2点)

(2) ア. being used 　　イ. to be using 　　ウ. to use 　　エ. using

(4) ア. another 　　イ. others 　　ウ. the other 　　エ. the others

(5) ア. considers 　　イ. grasps 　　ウ. has 　　エ. meets

3. 次の問いに英語で答えなさい。【内容についての思考力・判断力・表現力】　　(各4点)

(1) Just building water wells is not enough. So, what do we have to do?

_____

(2) Situations differ from place to place. So, what support do we have to provide?

_____

Sazae-san and Machiko Hasegawa Part 1

/50

A Translate the English into Japanese and the Japanese into English.【語彙の知識】(各1点)

1. cartoon 图 A1　　　[　　　　　　　] 　2. ＿＿＿＿＿＿＿＿ 動 B2　…に挿絵を入れる

3. ＿＿＿＿＿＿＿＿ 图 A2　フレーム, コマ　　4. ＿＿＿＿＿＿＿＿ 图 A2　エピソード, (1回分の)話

5. energetic 形 A2　　　[　　　　　　　] 　6. cheerfulness 图 B2　[　　　　　　　]

B Choose the word whose underlined part is pronounced differently from the other three.【発音の知識】(各2点)

1. ア. <u>a</u>nimated　　イ. ch<u>a</u>racter　　ウ. f<u>a</u>mily　　エ. fr<u>a</u>me

2. ア. <u>e</u>nergetic　　イ. <u>e</u>pisode　　ウ. <u>e</u>qual　　エ. m<u>e</u>mber

3. ア. app<u>ear</u>　　イ. ch<u>eer</u>fulness　　ウ. h<u>ear</u>d　　エ. y<u>ear</u>

C Complete the following English sentences to match the Japanese.【表現と文法の知識】

(各3点)

1. 私には2歳の息子がいます。

　 I have a (　　　　　　　) son.

2. 妻はスマートフォンで4コマ漫画を読むのが好きです。

　 My wife likes reading (　　　　　　　) comics on her smartphone.

3. この家は二世代家族用です。

　 This house is for a (　　　　　　) (　　　　　　　).

D Arrange the words in the proper order to match the Japanese.【表現と文法の知識・技能】

(各3点)

1. そのアーティストは, 慈善活動のために一連のコンサートを行った。

　 The artist gave (a / concerts / of / series) for charity.

＿＿＿＿＿＿＿＿＿＿＿＿＿＿＿＿＿＿＿＿＿＿＿＿＿＿＿＿＿＿

2. あなたの優しさが嬉しかった。

　 (happy / made / me / your kindness).

＿＿＿＿＿＿＿＿＿＿＿＿＿＿＿＿＿＿＿＿＿＿＿＿＿＿＿＿＿＿

3. これは有名な画家によって挿絵が描かれた本である。

　 This is (a book / a famous painter / by / illustrated).

＿＿＿＿＿＿＿＿＿＿＿＿＿＿＿＿＿＿＿＿＿＿＿＿＿＿＿＿＿＿

E Read the following passage and answer the questions below.

1 Do you know this woman? Maybe you have (1)(see) her on TV. She is Sazae, the main character in *Sazae-san*. *Sazae-san* is one of the most popular animated cartoons and (2)(by / is / loved / of / people) all ages. It (3)(based / is / on / the comic / with) the same title illustrated by Machiko Hasegawa.

2 *Sazae-san* originally appeared in a local newspaper in Kyushu as a series of four-frame comics in 1946. Each episode illustrates Sazae's daily life with her family members, friends and neighbors.

3 Sazae is a stay-at-home mom with a two-year-old son and (4)(live) in her parents' home with her three-generation family. She is an energetic and active woman. She is a little absent-minded and sometimes makes a lot of mistakes, but her (5) makes people around her happy.

1. 下線部(1), (4)の語を適切な形に変えなさい。【文法の知識】 (各2点)

   (1) _____

   (4) _____

2. 下線部(2), (3)の(　　)内の語句を適切に並べかえなさい。【表現と文法の知識】 (各3点)

   (2) _____

   (3) _____

3. 空所(5)に入る最も適当な語を選びなさい。【語彙の知識】 (2点)

   ア. cheered   イ. cheerful   ウ. cheerfully   エ. cheerfulness

4. 次の問いに英語で答えなさい。【内容についての思考力・判断力・表現力】 (各4点)

   (1) When did *Sazae-san* originally appear?

   _____

   (2) What does each episode of *Sazae-san* illustrate?

   _____

A Translate the English into Japanese and the Japanese into English.【語彙の知識】(各1点)

1. wise 形 A2　　　[　　　　　　] 2. ＿＿＿＿＿ 形 B2　控えめな，謙虚な

3. ＿＿＿＿＿ 形　しとやかな，上品な 4. ＿＿＿＿＿ 形 B1　忠実な，誠実な

5. relationship 名 B1　[　　　　　] 6. openly 副 B2　[　　　　　　]

B Choose the word whose underlined part is pronounced differently from the other three.【発音の知識】(各2点)

1. ア. <u>i</u>mage　　　イ. l<u>i</u>fe　　　ウ. w<u>i</u>fe　　　エ. w<u>i</u>se

2. ア. m<u>o</u>dest　　イ. m<u>o</u>tivate　　ウ. <u>o</u>penly　　エ. <u>ow</u>n

3. ア. <u>fa</u>ithful　イ. l<u>a</u>dylike　ウ. rel<u>a</u>tionship　エ. s<u>ai</u>d

C Complete the following English sentences to match the Japanese.【表現と文法の知識】

(各3点)

1. 息子はその秘密を守るという約束にずっと忠実である。

My son has (　　　　　) (　　　　　) (　　　　　) his promise to keep the secret.

2. 大谷翔平は偉大な選手であると同時に謙虚でもある。

Shohei Otani is (　　　　　), as well as a great player.

3. あなたらしく生きたほうがいい。

You should live your (　　　　　) way.

D Arrange the words in the proper order to match the Japanese.【表現と文法の知識・技能】

(各3点)

1. この建物は1,000年以上前に建てられたと考えられている。

It (built / is / that / this building / thought / was) more than 1,000 years ago.

2. シンガポールの経済は日本よりも速く成長している。

The economy of Singapore is (faster / growing / Japan / of / than / that).

3. 彼女は主人公を良き父として描いた。

She (a good father / as / described / the main character).

E Read the following passage and answer the questions below.

4 In the Showa era, a "good wife and wise mother" was the ideal image of Japanese women. It was thought that women should be modest, ladylike, and faithful to their husbands.

5 (1), Sazae has an equal relationship with her husband, Masuo. She is honest and always expresses her opinions openly and lives her own way. This (2)(a different image / from / is / of / that) most Japanese women at that time.

6 Machiko Hasegawa once said, "I (3)(laugh / many people / to / want) every day." She also said, "If there is a woman who is always cheerful and honest, (4)she can motivate those around her to make the world brighter." She hoped many people would lead a happy life, so she described Sazae as her ideal image of a cheerful and honest woman.

1. 空所(1)に入る最も適当な語(句)を選びなさい。【語彙・表現の知識】　　　　　　（3点）

　　ア. As a result　　　イ. First　　　　ウ. For example　　エ. On the other hand

2. 下線部(2), (3)の（　　）内の語句を適切に並べかえなさい。【表現の知識】　　　　（各3点）

　　(2) _____

　　(3) _____

3. 下線部(4)は何を指していますか。本文中から抜き出して答えなさい。

　　　　　　　　　　　　　　　　【内容についての思考力・判断力・表現力】（3点）

_____

4. 次の問いに英語で答えなさい。【内容についての思考力・判断力・表現力】　　　　（各4点）

　　(1) What was the ideal image of Japanese women in the Showa era?

_____

　　(2) What was Machiko's ideal image of a woman?

_____

A Translate the English into Japanese and the Japanese into English.【語彙の知識】（各1点）

1. tomboyish 形　　　[　　　　　　] 2. _____ 名 B1　生徒，弟子

3. _____ 名　　デビュー　　　　4. _____ 名 B1　アニメーション

5. cartoonist 名　　[　　　　　] 6. chauvinism 名　　[　　　　　　]

B Choose the word which has primary stress on a different syllable from the other three.【アクセントの知識】　　　　　　　　　　　　　　　　　（各2点）

1. ア. faith-ful　　　イ. mod-est　　　ウ. pu-pil　　　エ. up-on

2. ア. car-toon-ist　イ. ep-i-sode　　ウ. il-lus-trate　エ. tom-boy-ish

3. ア. an-i-ma-tion　イ. en-er-get-ic　ウ. in-de-pend-ent　エ. pro-fes-sion-al

C Complete the following English sentences to match the Japanese.【表現と文法の知識】

（各3点）

1. 時間があれば，この書類を見てくれ。

If you have time, (　　　　　　) (　　　　　　) (　　　　　) at this document.

2. どうやってそんなに素晴らしいアイデアを思いついたの？

How did you (　　　　　) (　　　　　　) such a great idea?

3. その野球選手は，2018年に国際的なデビューを果たした。

The baseball player (　　　　　　) his international (　　　　　) in 2018.

D Arrange the words in the proper order to match the Japanese.【表現と文法の知識・技能】

（各3点）

1. 彼の妻だけでなく，ケンもその事故を目撃した。

Ken (as / as / his wife / saw / well) the accident.

_____

2. 先生に手伝ってもらうように頼んだらどうですか。

Why don't you (ask / help / to / you / your teacher)?

_____

3. 運転しながらスマートフォンを使ってはいけません。

Don't (driving / use / while / your smartphone).

_____

E Read the following passage and answer the questions below.

Machiko Hasegawa

1920	She was born in Saga. She was a bright and tomboyish girl. She liked drawing pictures.
1934	She became a private pupil of manga artist Suihou Tagawa. At the age of 15, she made her debut (1) a manga artist.
1946	The local newspaper in Kyushu asked her to contribute a series of four-frame comics. She (2)(an idea / hit / included / that / upon) the main characters of *Sazae-san* while walking on a nearby beach.
1947	She (3)(found) her own publishing company with her sisters in order to publish *Sazae-san* herself.
1969	*Sazae-san* (4)(begin) as a TV animation.
1992	She (5)(at / away / of / passed / the age) 72 and received the People's Honor Award in the same year.

　Machiko was the first female professional cartoonist in Japan. She was a strong and independent woman. Machiko, as well as Sazae, was an energetic and active woman in the Showa era.

1. 空所(1)に入る最も適当な語を選びなさい。【語彙の知識】　　　　　　　　　（2点）

　　ア. as　　　　　　　イ. for　　　　　　ウ. in　　　　　　エ. to

2. 下線部(2), (5)の(　　　)内の語句を適切に並べかえなさい。【表現の知識】　　（各3点）

　　(2) ....

　　(5) ....

3. 下線部(3), (4)の語を適切な形に変えなさい。【語彙の知識】　　　　　　　　（各2点）

　　(3) ....

　　(4) ....

4. 次の問いに英語で答えなさい。【内容についての思考力・判断力・表現力】　　（各4点）

　　(1) What did the local newspaper in Kyushu ask Machiko Hasegawa to do?

　　..

　　(2) When was the People's Honor Award given to Machiko?

　　..

A Lover of the Slums of Ghana — Part 1

A Translate the English into Japanese and the Japanese into English. 【語彙の知識】(各1点)

1. dump 图 B1 [   ]   2. _____ 图   スラム街
3. _____ 图   墓場, 廃棄場   4. _____ 動 B2   …を抽出する
5. poisonous 形 B1 [   ]   6. discard 動 [   ]

B Choose the word whose underlined part is pronounced differently from the other three. 【発音の知識】(各2点)

1. ア. an<u>i</u>mation　イ. descr<u>i</u>be　ウ. d<u>i</u>scard　エ. ep<u>i</u>sode
2. ア. c<u>o</u>mfortable　イ. d<u>u</u>mp　ウ. extr<u>a</u>ct　エ. sl<u>u</u>m
3. ア. br<u>ea</u>the　イ. d<u>e</u>sperately　ウ. el<u>e</u>ctronic　エ. m<u>e</u>tal

C Complete the following English sentences to match the Japanese. 【表現と文法の知識】(各3点)

1. 机の引き出しの中を整理していて, 私はこの古い写真を偶然見つけました。
   Cleaning out my desk drawer, I came (   ) this old picture.
2. この雑誌は取っておきたいの。捨てないでね。
   I want to keep these magazines. Please don't (   ) them away.
3. 彼は実業家として成功したが, それは家庭生活を犠牲にしたものだった。
   He was a successful businessman, but it was (   ) the expense (   ) his family life.

D Arrange the words in the proper order to match the Japanese. 【表現と文法の知識・技能】(各3点)

1. 彼女は, 給料が出たら買うものを探しながら, たくさんの店を見て回る。
   She browses a lot of stores, (buy / for / looking / things / to) when she receives her paycheck.

2. 肉と皮のために狩猟されて, アメリカバイソンはほとんど絶滅しかけた。
   (and / caught / for / killed / their meat) and skins, buffaloes were almost extinct.

3. 3週間入院した後, また自分の家に戻ることができてルースはうれしかった。
   After three weeks in the hospital, Luth was glad (back / be / her own home / in / to).

E Read the following passage and answer the questions below.

1 Mago Nagasaka, a street painter, came across a photo in 2016. In the photo, a child was standing in a dump site overseas. (1)(by / of / shocked / the realities / the world's waste), in 2017 he visited a slum in Ghana which was described as the world's largest "graveyard" for electronic devices.

2 (2)There, young people were living desperately, burning the electronic devices to melt and extract the metals inside them. Those devices had been thrown away by people in developed countries and then dumped in Ghana. Many of those young people breathed in too much poisonous gas, got cancer, and died in their thirties. Mago was astonished to know that he was leading a comfortable life at the expense of their lives.

3 "I'm going to spread (3)this fact to developed countries through the power of art," said Mago. So, he started to create artworks (4)(by / discarded / electronic waste (e-waste) / in / using) Ghana and sold them.

1. 下線部(1), (4)の( )内の語句を適切に並べかえなさい。【表現と文法の知識】　　（各3点）

(1) _____

(4) _____

2. 下線部(2)はどこを指していますか。日本語で答えなさい。【内容についての思考力・判断力・表現力】

（3点）

_____

3. 下線部(3)の具体的な内容を，日本語で答えなさい。【内容についての思考力・判断力・表現力】　　（3点）

_____

4. 次の問いに英語で答えなさい。【内容についての思考力・判断力・表現力】　　（各4点）

(1) Where did the discarded devices in a slum in Ghana come from?

_____

(2) Why did many young people in the slum die of cancer in their thirties?

_____

A Translate the English into Japanese and the Japanese into English.【語彙の知識】（各1点）

1. economic 形 B1 [   ]
2. _____ 名 B1 成長，発展
3. foster 動 [   ]
4. _____ 形 B1 有望な，希望が持てる
5. hire 動 B1 [   ]
6. _____ 代 B1 誰も…ない

B Choose the word which has primary stress on a different syllable from the other three.【アクセントの知識】（各2点）

1. ア. fos-ter   イ. hope-ful   ウ. prof-it   エ. pro-mote
2. ア. dan-ger-ous イ. mu-se-um   ウ. poi-son-ous エ. tom-boy-ish
3. ア. a-rith-me-tic イ. e-co-nom-ic ウ. fa-cil-i-ty   エ. sus-tain-a-ble

C Complete the following English sentences to match the Japanese.【表現と文法の知識】（各3点）

1. 生きている限り，私たちの心臓は鼓動をやめることは決してない。
   As (   ) as we live, our hearts will never stop beating.
2. 彼は自分自身の命を危険にさらしてその少女を救助した。
   He rescued the girl at the (   ) of his own life.
3. 彼は車庫を子供たちの遊び部屋に変えるつもりです。
   He is going to turn the garage (   ) a playroom for the children.

D Arrange the words in the proper order to match the Japanese.【表現と文法の知識・技能】（各3点）

1. 暑い気候の地に住む人々がカレーのような辛いものを食べるのは奇妙だ。
   It is strange that people (eat / hot climates / hot foods / in / like) curry.

2. 国際連合はこの地域に平和をもたらす重い責任がある。
   The UN has (a heavy responsibility / bringing / for / peace / to) this region.

3. 私は町の4軒の本屋に行ってみたが，欲しかった本はどこにも置いてなかった。
   I went to four bookstores in town, but (had / none / of / the book / them) I wanted.

E Read the following passage and answer the questions below.

4 Mago believes that sustainable economic growth is important. So, he has used the profits from his artworks to promote (1)it from the following perspectives: education, culture and economy.

5 In 2018, Mago started the first school in the slum, "MAGO ART AND STUDY." It will (2)be (   ) to attend as long as Mago lives. Children learn subjects like English and arithmetic there.

6 In August 2019, Mago founded the "MAGO E-Waste Museum," the first cultural facility in the slums. He believes that the museum will help to bring (3) and new jobs, and foster a hopeful new society.

7 Mago has set (4)(a state-of-the-art recycling plant / building / his sights / in / on) Ghana. He is going to hire people from the slums to work in his factory. (5)That way, none of the local people will need to do dangerous work at the risk of their health. Mago hopes to turn the graveyard of e-waste into a zero-pollution sustainable town.

1. 下線部(1)は何を指していますか。英語で答えなさい。【内容についての思考力・判断力・表現力】（2点）

—————————————————————————————————————

2. 下線部(2)が「無料である」という意味になるように，（   ）に適語を補いなさい。【表現の知識】
（2点）

　　be (   )

3. 空所(3)に入る最も適当な語を選びなさい。【語彙と表現の知識】　　　　　　　　（2点）
　　ア. culture　　　　　イ. economy　　　　ウ. education　　　エ. factory

4. 下線部(4)の(   )内の語句を適切に並べかえなさい。【表現と文法の知識】　　　　（3点）

—————————————————————————————————————

5. 下線部(5)の具体的な内容を，日本語で答えなさい。【内容についての思考力・判断力・表現力】　（3点）

—————————————————————————————————————

6. 次の問いに英語で答えなさい。【内容についての思考力・判断力・表現力】　　　　　（各4点）
　（1）What did Mago do from the perspective of promoting education?

—————————————————————————————————————

　（2）What does Mago hope to do by building the most advanced recycling plant in Ghana?

—————————————————————————————————————

A Translate the English into Japanese and the Japanese into English.【語彙の知識】(各1点)

1. ＿＿＿＿＿＿ 名 B1 タブレット
2. ＿＿＿＿＿＿ 名 B2 製造業者, メーカー
3. ＿＿＿＿＿＿ 名 B2 処分, ごみ処理
4. usable 形 [   ]
5. individually 副 [   ]
6. collectively 副 [   ]

B Choose the word whose underlined part is pronounced differently from the other three.【発音の知識】 (各2点)

1. ア. dispo<u>s</u>al   イ. <u>fo</u>ster   ウ. gr<u>ow</u>th   エ. h<u>o</u>peful
2. ア. devi<u>c</u>e   イ. expre<u>ss</u>   ウ. relea<u>s</u>e   エ. u<u>s</u>able
3. ア. attra<u>c</u>tive   イ. e-w<u>a</u>ste   ウ. manufa<u>c</u>turer エ. ta<u>b</u>let

C Complete the following English sentences to match the Japanese.【表現と文法の知識】

(各3点)

1. ランナーたちが次々とスタジアムに戻ってきた。

   Runners returned to the stadium (   ) after (   ).

2. これらのコップは割れやすいので, 注意して洗わなくてはいけない。

   Since these glasses are fragile, you must wash them (   ) care.

3. 木曜日か金曜日にあなたにお会いできます。

   I can meet you (   ) Thursday (   ) Friday.

D Arrange the words in the proper order to match the Japanese.【表現と文法の知識・技能】

(各3点)

1. その少女は, おもちゃ遊びをして何時間も楽しく過ごします。

   The little girl amuses (by / for / herself / hours / playing) with her toys.

2. 彼女は職場へ出かける前にアパートのドアに鍵をかけた。

   She locked (before / for / leaving / her apartment door / work).

3. あの学校には, 男の子はワイシャツを着てネクタイをすることを求める服装規定がある。

   That school has (a dress code / boys / requiring / to / wear) shirts and ties.

E Read the following passage and answer the questions below.

Kumi: What do you think about the e-waste problem?

Takashi: New smartphones and tablets are released one after another. They look very attractive. But we have to (1)think twice before buying a new device. We should ask ourselves if we really need a new one.

Kumi: I agree with you, Takashi. In addition, once we've got a device, we have to (2)use it until it no longer works. We have to treat it with care. It's also important to repair and reuse our devices.

Vivian: Exactly. We consumers should become more aware of the e-waste problem. (3)Also, I think the manufacturers should be responsible for disposal of their products when they are no longer usable.

Takashi: You have a good point! Governments should require the manufacturers (4)(by / collect / e-waste / setting up / to) collection centers or take-back systems, either individually or collectively.

Kumi: Great.

1. 下線部(1)の具体的な内容を，日本語で答えなさい。【内容についての思考力・判断力・表現力】　（3点）

....

2. 下線部(2)を実現するための方法を，日本語で答えなさい。

【内容についての思考力・判断力・表現力】（3点）

....

3. 下線部(3)は何に対して何を追加していますか。日本語で答えなさい。

【内容についての思考力・判断力・表現力】（3点）

....

4. 下線部(4)の(　　)内の語句を適切に並べかえなさい。【表現と文法の知識】　（3点）

....

5. 次の問いに英語で答えなさい。【内容についての思考力・判断力・表現力】　（各4点）

(1) What should consumers do about the e-waste problem?

....

(2) What responsibility do the manufacturers have?

....

To Achieve Gender Equality Part 1

/50

A Translate the English into Japanese and the Japanese into English.【語彙の知識】(各1点)

1. rank 動 [   ]　　2. _____ 名 フォーラム, 公開討論

3. _____ 名 B1 政治, 政界　　4. _____ 名 B2 議会

5. wage 名 B2 [   ]　　6. rate 名 A2 [   ]

B Choose the word which has primary stress on a different syllable from the other three.【アクセントの知識】 (各2点)

1. ア. be-tween　　イ. fo-rum　　ウ. gen-der　　エ. wel-fare

2. ア. in-flu-ence　　イ. par-lia-ment　　ウ. pol-i-tics　　エ. re-gard-ing

3. ア. e-co-nom-ic　　イ. e-lim-i-nate　　ウ. en-vi-ron-ment　　エ. e-qual-i-ty

C Complete the following English sentences to match the Japanese.【表現と文法の知識】

(各3点)

1. 男女平等は平和で持続可能な世界のために必要不可欠である。

(   ) (   ) is essential for a peaceful and sustainable world.

2. 彼は私たちの計画に関しては何も言わなかった。

He said nothing (   ) our plan.

3. 私の夫は3ヶ月の育休を取った。

My husband took a three-month (   ) (   ).

D Arrange the words in the proper order to match the Japanese.【表現と文法の知識・技能】

(各3点)

1. 私たちは湖の近くにあるレストランで食事をした。

We ate (a restaurant / at / located / the lake / near).

_____

2. その芸術家は油絵の発展に大きな影響を与えた。

The artist (a major influence / had / on / the development) of oil painting.

_____

3. この航空会社は世界でベスト5にランクインしている。

This airline (among / been / has / ranked) the five best airlines in the world.

_____

E Read the following passage and answer the questions below.

1 Iceland is a Nordic island country located in the North Atlantic Ocean, with a population of about 350,000. The country has been ranked first in gender equality by the World Economic Forum for over ten years. (1)(an active role / are / how / playing / women) in Icelandic society?

2 In Iceland, more women are active in politics than in many other countries. About 40% of the members of parliament are women. Women have a major influence on policy making (2) welfare, education and wages.

3 In addition, the employment rate of women in Iceland is higher than 80%. There is a good working environment for women, and many working mothers take their babies to work with (3)them. The childcare leave system is well developed, and a high percentage of men (4) women take childcare leave. Many companies are also trying to eliminate the wage gap between men and women. Iceland may be the best place in the world (5)(for / have / who / women / working) children.

1. 下線部(1), (5)の(　　)内の語句を適切に並べかえなさい。【表現と文法の知識】　　　　（各3点）

　　(1) _____

　　(5) _____

2. 空所(2), (4)に入る最も適当な語(句)を選びなさい。【語彙と表現の知識】　　　　（各2点）

　　(2) ア. regard　　　　イ. regarded　　　　ウ. regarding　　　　エ. regardless

　　(4) ア. as many as　　イ. as well as　　　ウ. in spite of　　　エ. instead of

3. 下線部(3)が指すものを, 本文中から抜き出しなさい。【内容についての思考力・判断力・表現力】（2点）

　　_____

4. 次の問いに英語で答えなさい。【内容についての思考力・判断力・表現力】　　　　（各4点）

　　(1) Where is Iceland located?

　　_____

　　(2) How high is the employment rate of women in Iceland?

　　_____

A Translate the English into Japanese and the Japanese into English.【語彙の知識】(各1点)

1. _____ 名 B2 （専業）主婦
2. _____ 名 B1 収入，所得
3. _____ 形 B2 不満な
4. protest 動 B2 [   ]
5. inequality 名 [   ]
6. institution 名 B2 [   ]

B Choose the word whose underlined part is pronounced differently from the other three.【発音の知識】(各2点)

1. ア. dev<u>e</u>lop   イ. <u>e</u>lect   ウ. f<u>e</u>male   エ. prot<u>e</u>st
2. ア. ch<u>i</u>ldcare   イ. housew<u>i</u>fe   ウ. <u>i</u>ncome   エ. str<u>i</u>ke
3. ア. diss<u>a</u>tisfied   イ. g<u>a</u>p   ウ. gr<u>a</u>dually   エ. inequ<u>a</u>lity

C Complete the following English sentences to match the Japanese.【表現と文法の知識】

(各3点)

1. 何千人もの人々が電気料金の値上げに抗議をした。

Thousands of people (   ) (   ) the increase in electricity charges.

2. 彼女はそのメイン料理に不満のように見えた。

She looked (   ) (   ) the main dish.

3. 彼らは昇給を求めてストライキを行った。

They (   ) (   ) (   ) for a raise.

D Arrange the words in the proper order to match the Japanese.【表現と文法の知識・技能】

(各3点)

1. 最低賃金は30年前よりずっと上がっている。

The minimum wage (higher / is / much / than) it was 30 years ago.

_____

2. 日本では高校生が自転車で通学するのは普通だ。

In Japan, it is (for / to / common / high school students) go to school by bike.

_____

3. その建物は以前は大きな映画館だった。

(be / the building / to / used) a big movie theater.

_____

E Read the following passage and answer the questions below.

4 How has Iceland achieved gender equality? In Iceland, (1)it used to be common for women to do housework and childcare as full-time housewives. Even if they were working, women's income was much lower than men's. Women felt dissatisfied with such a situation.

5 On October 24, 1975, about 90% of adult females in Iceland went on strike to protest against gender inequality in their workplaces and families. On that day, (2)they boycotted all their work and housework, and gathered together in a square in the capital city, Reykjavik. The strike (3)(made / realize / that / the men / they) could not live a single day without women.

6 As a result of the strike, Icelandic society started to change. In 1980, the first female president was elected. Social institutions and laws for gender equality were developed. The working conditions for women also improved, and the wage gap was gradually reduced. These movements toward gender equality (4)(Iceland / in / making / succeeded / what) it is now.

1. 下線部(1)，(2)が指すものを本文中から抜き出しなさい。【内容についての思考力・判断力・表現力】

(各3点)

(1) ....

(2) ....

2. 下線部(3)，(4)の（　　）内の語句を適切に並べかえなさい。【表現と文法の知識】　　（各3点）

(3) ....

(4) ....

3. 次の問いに英語で答えなさい。【内容についての思考力・判断力・表現力】　　（各4点）

(1) Why did women in Iceland go on strike in 1975?

....

(2) When was the first female president elected in Iceland?

....

A Translate the English into Japanese and the Japanese into English.【語彙の知識】（各1点）

1. disparity 名 [   ] 2. ＿＿＿＿＿＿ 動 B2 …の量を計る

3. ＿＿＿＿＿＿ 動 B2 …を評価する 4. ＿＿＿＿＿＿ 名 B1 経済状態，経済面

5. urgent 形 B1 [   ] 6. continuous 形 B1 [   ]

B Choose the word whose underlined part is pronounced differently from the other three.【発音の知識】 （各2点）

1. ア. dis<u>a</u>rity   イ. ev<u>a</u>luate   ウ. r<u>a</u>nking   エ. w<u>a</u>ge

2. ア. reg<u>ar</u>ding   イ. <u>ur</u>gent   ウ. w<u>or</u>k   エ. w<u>or</u>ld

3. ア. c<u>o</u>ntinuous   イ. envir<u>o</u>nment   ウ. p<u>o</u>litical   エ. partic<u>u</u>larly

C Complete the following English sentences to match the Japanese.【表現と文法の知識】

（各3点）

1. 10人に3人の中学生はスマートフォンを持っていないらしい。

It seems that three (   ) (   ) ten junior high school students do not have a smartphone.

2. 私たちはその新薬の効果を適切に評価する必要がある。

We need to (   ) the effect of the new medicine properly.

3. その政党は新たな候補を指名した。

The (   ) party nominated the new candidate.

D Arrange the words in the proper order to match the Japanese.【表現と文法の知識・技能】

（各3点）

1. 彼はその数学の問題を解くことに成功した。

He (in / solving / succeeded / the math problem).

2. その地域に住む人々は，その問題に対して根強い怒りを持っている。

People living in the area (anger / deeply / have / rooted) about the issue.

3. 私の娘は，自分で生計を立てようと努力している。

My daughter (earn / efforts / is / making / to) her own living.

E Read the following passage and answer the questions below.

Japan 120th in Global Gender Equality Ranking

Japan has (1)(gender inequality rates / in / of / one / the highest) the world. In the World Economic Forum's Global Gender Equality Ranking in 2021, Japan's scorecard was 120 out of 156 countries. This ranking was the lowest of the G7 countries. (2), Nordic countries, including Iceland, were at the top of the list.

Why does Japan have such a low ranking? In the Global Gender Equality Ranking, gender disparity is quantified and evaluated in four areas: politics, economics, education and health. The gender gap in Japan is particularly large, especially in the political and economic fields. The involvement of women in (3)these fields is an urgent issue.

The Japanese government is trying to encourage gender equality but we are not succeeding in achieving (4)it. We should learn from Nordic countries and try to change deeply rooted social practices. We must have a clear goal — to create a better working environment for both women and men — and make continuous efforts to realize it for ourselves.

1. 下線部(1)の(　)内の語句を適切に並べかえなさい。【表現の知識】　　　　（3点）

2. 空所(2)に入る最も適当な語句を選びなさい。【語彙と表現の知識】　　　　（3点）

　　ア. As a result　　イ. For example　　ウ. In addition　　エ. On the other hand

3. 下線部(3), (4)が指すものを本文中から抜き出しなさい。【内容についての思考力・判断力・表現力】

（各3点）

　　(3)

　　(4)

4. 次の問いに英語で答えなさい。【内容についての思考力・判断力・表現力】　　　　（各4点）

　　(1) In what areas is gender disparity evaluated?

　　(2) Why is it difficult to encourage gender equality in Japan?

A Translate the English into Japanese and the Japanese into English. 【語彙の知識】（各1点）

1. ＿＿＿＿＿＿ 图 B1 ドキュメンタリー　　2. ＿＿＿＿＿＿ 图　（魚の）乱獲

3. highlight 動 B1　[　　　　　]　　4. exponentially 副　[　　　　　]

5. excessively 副　[　　　　　]　　6. ＿＿＿＿＿＿ 图 B2　飢餓，餓死

B Choose the word which has primary stress on a different syllable from the other three. 【アクセントの知識】

（各2点）

1. ア. de-crease (動詞)　イ. im-pact　　ウ. im-ply　　エ. pre-dict

2. ア. de-mand　　　　イ. high-light　ウ. mes-sage　エ. spe-cies

3. ア. con-tin-ue　　　イ. over-fish-ing　ウ. pol-i-tics　エ. star-va-tion

C Complete the following English sentences to match the Japanese. 【表現と文法の知識】

（各3点）

1. 恐竜は何百万年も前に絶滅した。

Dinosaurs died (　　　　　　) millions of years ago.

2. バーミンガムは英国最大の都市の一つである。

Birmingham is (　　　　　　) the largest cities in Britain.

3. 夏になると，エアコンのために電気の需要は倍増する。

In summer, the (　　　　　) (　　　　　) electricity doubles because of air conditioning.

D Arrange the words in the proper order to match the Japanese. 【表現と文法の知識・技能】

（各3点）

1. 川端康成は，ノーベル文学賞を受賞した最初の日本人作家だった。

Yasunari Kawabata was (awarded / be / the first Japanese writer / the Nobel Prize in Literature / to).

＿＿＿＿＿＿＿＿＿＿＿＿＿＿＿＿＿＿＿＿＿＿＿＿＿＿

2. どうして私が言ったようにそれをしなかったのですか。

Why didn't you do it (as / I / to / told / you) do it?

＿＿＿＿＿＿＿＿＿＿＿＿＿＿＿＿＿＿＿＿＿＿＿＿＿＿

3. 航空会社のパイロットになるという彼女の夢は実現しそうだ。

Her dream of becoming an airline pilot (come / is / likely / to / true).

＿＿＿＿＿＿＿＿＿＿＿＿＿＿＿＿＿＿＿＿＿＿＿＿＿＿

E Read the following passage and answer the questions below.

Imagine an ocean without fish. Imagine your meals without any seafood. This is the future if we do not think seriously and act soon.

(1)This is the message which the film titled *The End of the Line* gives us. The film is the world's first major documentary to focus (2) the impact of overfishing on the world's oceans. Scientists predict that if we continue to fish (3) we are doing now, we will see the end of most seafood by 2048.

The film highlights how many well-known species are likely to die out. (4), bluefin tuna are among them. In Spain, the catch of bluefin tuna has exponentially decreased: 5,000 million tons in 1999, 2,000 million tons in 2000, and 900 million tons in 2005. (5), they are still being caught excessively because of the increasing demand for sushi in Western countries. The film implies that a world with no fish will experience mass starvation.

1. 下線部(1)の具体的な内容を，日本語で答えなさい。【内容についての思考力・判断力・表現力】 （4点）

2. 空所(2)～(5)に入る最も適当な語(句)を選びなさい。【語彙と表現の知識】 （各2点）

    (2) ア. at   イ. for   ウ. on   エ. to

    (3) ア. as   イ. even if   ウ. unless   エ. while

    (4) ア. As a result   イ. For example   ウ. In addition   エ. In short

    (5) ア. However   イ. Instead   ウ. Moreover   エ. Therefore

3. 次の問いに英語で答えなさい。【内容についての思考力・判断力・表現力】 （各4点）

    (1) What does *The End of the Line* emphasize so that people pay special attention to overfishing?

    (2) What does the film suggest?

A World with No Fish

Part 2

/50

A Translate the English into Japanese and the Japanese into English.【語彙の知識】（各1点）

1. destructive 形 B1　　[　　　　　　　]
2. ＿＿＿＿＿＿＿＿ 形 B2　見えない，目につかない
3. ＿＿＿＿＿＿＿＿ 副 B2　皮肉にも　　
4. ＿＿＿＿＿＿＿＿ 動　…の位置を定める
5. shoal 名　　　　[　　　　　　　]
6. quantity 名 B1　　[　　　　　　　]

B Choose the word which has primary stress on a different syllable from the other three.【アクセントの知識】　　　　　　　　　　　　　　　　　　　（各2点）

1. ア. find-er　　　　イ. im-prove　　　　ウ. rhi-no　　　　エ. so-nar
2. ア. con-trib-ute　　イ. de-struc-tive　　ウ. po-si-tion　　エ. quan-ti-ty
3. ア. di-men-sion-al　イ. in-vis-i-ble　　ウ. par-tic-u-lar　エ. se-ri-ous-ly

C Complete the following English sentences to match the Japanese.【表現と文法の知識】

（各3点）

1. 食事はすべておいしかったが，特にスープはとてもおいしかった。

   All meals were good, but the soup in (　　　　　　　　) was delicious.
2. 私たちには，その計画を実行するのに十分なお金がありません。

   We don't have enough money to (　　　　　　　) out the plan.
3. 私たちのオフィスには高性能のコンピュータが2台備えられています。

   Our office is equipped (　　　　　　　) two powerful computers.

D Arrange the words in the proper order to match the Japanese.【表現と文法の知識・技能】

（各3点）

1. 息子は，豆腐がいかに健康に良いかをようやく認識し始めている。

   My son is finally beginning to (healthy / how / is / realize / tofu).

2. 私が今言って聞かせたことを覚えておきなさい。大きくなったらとても大切になるから。

   Remember (just / I've / told / what / you). It'll be very important when you grow up.

3. あなたは服装にもっと気をつけなければならない。

   You need to (attention / more / pay / to / your clothes).

E Read the following passage and answer the questions below.

Fishing with modern technology is one of the most destructive activities on earth. (1)Trawling, in particular, is very harmful. To understand how harmful it actually is, let's compare trawling for fish in the ocean to carrying out the same practice on land. Imagine a huge net sweeping across the plains of Africa and catching lions, elephants and rhinos. It also pulls out every plant and tree.

Such destructive activity is carried out every day in every sea and ocean across the world. People, however, pay little attention to what is happening under the sea (2) it is invisible.

Technology in the fishing industry has advanced. Ironically, however, (3)this has contributed to overfishing. The Global Positioning System and sonars are used in fish finders. They can (4) the locations of a shoal of fish underwater, (5) information about their quantity, and even (6) three-dimensional images. Fishing boats are now equipped with improved engines, nets and lines.

1. 下線部(1)の理由を，日本語で答えなさい。【内容についての思考力・判断力・表現力】　　　（3点）

2. 空所(2)に入る最も適当な語を選びなさい。【語彙の知識，内容についての思考力・判断力・表現力】　（3点）
　　ア. because　　　　イ. if　　　　　　ウ. though　　　　エ. when

3. 下線部(3)は何を指していますか。日本語で答えなさい。【内容についての思考力・判断力・表現力】（3点）

4. 空所(4)～(6)に入る最も適当な語をそれぞれ選びなさい。【語彙の知識】　　　　　（各1点）
　　ア. cause　　　　イ. find　　　　　ウ. give　　　　エ. make
　　(4) (　　　　) 　　(5) (　　　　) 　　(6) (　　　　)

5. 次の問いに英語で答えなさい。【内容についての思考力・判断力・表現力】　　　　　（各4点）
　　(1) What does the writer want us to do by imagining a huge net sweeping across the plains of Africa?

　　(2) What are some examples of advanced technology used to find fish?

A Translate the English into Japanese and the Japanese into English.【語彙の知識】(各1点)

1. _____ 動 B1 …を無視する
2. _____ 名 割り当て量, 取り分
3. marine 形 B1 [   ]
4. _____ 名 B1 保護区
5. certified 形 [   ]
6. fishery 名 [   ]

B Choose the word which has primary stress on a different syllable from the other three.【アクセントの知識】(各2点)

1. ア. au-thor   イ. ig-nore   ウ. quo-ta   エ. re-source
2. ア. cer-ti-fied   イ. fish-er-y   ウ. pos-si-ble   エ. so-lu-tion
3. ア. il-le-gal-ly   イ. pol-i-ti-cian   ウ. re-spon-si-ble   エ. sus-tain-a-ble

C Complete the following English sentences to match the Japanese.【表現と文法の知識】

(各3点)

1. 私は彼女にこんにちはと言ったのに, まったく無視された。

   I said hello to her, but she completely (   ) me.

2. 先生は宿題を増やすことで, その生徒の成績が悪いのに対応した。

   The teacher reacted (   ) the student's bad grades by giving him more homework.

3. 私はレポートのコピーを部屋にいたすべての人に渡しました。

   I passed copies of my report (   ) everyone in the room.

D Arrange the words in the proper order to match the Japanese.【表現と文法の知識・技能】

(各3点)

1. 彼女は何が起こっているのかなかなか理解できなかった。

   She (rather / realize / slow / to / was) what was going on.

   _____

2. 宇宙に星が実際にどのくらいあるかはわかっていない。

   (in / of / space / stars / the actual number) is not known.

   _____

3. 飛行機で座席が私の隣になった男性はずっとしゃべり続けた。

   The man who (I / next / on / sitting / to / was) the plane talked all the time.

   _____

E Read the following passage and answer the questions below.

Who is responsible (1) the situation? Consumers buy endangered fish (2) thinking about the impact (3) the environment. Politicians ignore the advice and warnings (4) scientists. Fishermen break quotas and fish illegally. The global fishing industry is slow to react to the disaster so near at hand.

The documentary *The End of the Line* shows simple and possible (5) for this international problem. Every country needs to control fishing by reducing the number of fishing boats across the world. We should protect large areas of the ocean as marine reserves. Consumers should buy fish only from certified sustainable fisheries.

"Overfishing is one of the great environmental disasters," said one of the film producers. "I hope the film will change our lifestyles and what we eat." Charles Clover, the author of (6)(based / is / the book / the film / which) on, says, "We must act now to protect the sea from overfishing in order to pass rich marine resources to the next generation."

1. 空所(1)〜(4)に入る最も適当な語をそれぞれ選びなさい。【語彙と表現の知識】　　　　（各1点）

　　ア. for　　　　　　イ. from　　　　　ウ. on　　　　　　エ. without

　　(1) (　　　　　)　　(2) (　　　　　)　　(3) (　　　　　)　　(4) (　　　　　)

2. 空所(5)に入る最も適当な語を選びなさい。【語彙の知識】　　　　　　　　　　　　（3点）

　　ア. explanations　　イ. facts　　　　ウ. reasons　　　　エ. solutions

3. 下線部(6)の(　　　)内の語句を適切に並べかえなさい。【表現と文法の知識】　　　　（3点）

4. 次の問いに英語で答えなさい。【内容についての思考力・判断力・表現力】　　　　　（各5点）

　　(1) What does each country need to do to control fishing?

　　(2) What should consumers do to contribute to solving the problem of overfishing?

A World with No Fish

Part 4 /50

A Translate the English into Japanese and the Japanese into English.【語彙の知識】(各1点)

1. analysis 名 B1   [   ]   2. _____ 名 B1   意向，意志

3. _____ 動 B2   …を行う   4. _____ 名   (映画などの)初日，封切り

5. indicate 動 A2   [   ]   6. profound 形   [   ]

B Choose the word which has primary stress on a different syllable from the other three.【アクセントの知識】(各2点)

1. ア. con-duct（動詞） イ. pre-miere ウ. pro-found エ. sur-vey（名詞）

2. ア. foun-da-tion イ. in-di-cate ウ. in-ten-tion エ. per-cent-age

3. ア. a-nal-y-sis イ. cer-e-mo-ny ウ. con-se-quent-ly エ. des-per-ate-ly

C Complete the following English sentences to match the Japanese.【表現と文法の知識】(各3点)

1. 昨日私に何が起きたか聞きましたか。

Did you hear what (   ) (   ) me yesterday?

2. 彼らは結婚するつもりがありませんでした。

They had no (   ) to get married.

3. 値段は倍になりました。去年は10ドルでしたが今年は20ドルです。

The price has (   ): last year it was $10 and this year it's $20.

D Arrange the words in the proper order to match the Japanese.【表現と文法の知識・技能】(各3点)

1. ここで働く人の90パーセントが男性です。

(ninety / of / percent / the people / who) work here are men.

_____

2. あなたが正しいと信じることをしなさい。

Do what (be / believe / right / to / you).

_____

3. 私はとても疲れていました。目を開けていようとがんばったのですが，できませんでした。

I was very tired. I (keep / my eyes / open / to / tried), but I couldn't.

_____

E Read the following passage and answer the questions below.

Does the film affect consumer attitudes and intentions?

A survey was conducted before and after the film's premiere in theaters. Before watching the film, 26% of these audiences indicated that they did not believe overfishing to be a serious problem. (1)(after / happened / this group / to / what) watching the film? Eighty-five percent of them answered that it was quite a big problem.

The audiences were also asked about their buying habits before the film and their intended buying habits after the film. The percentage of the audiences who (2)(buy / had / only sustainable fish / the intention / to) almost doubled from 43% to 84%.

(3)The impact was even more profound on the group who (4)were not aware of the problems of overfishing. Only 17% of this group bought sustainable fish before watching the film. However, after watching, 82% said they would now try to buy sustainable fish.

1. 下線部(1), (2)の(　　)内の語句を適切に並べかえなさい。【表現と文法の知識】　　（各3点）

   (1) _____

   (2) _____

2. 下線部(3)の内容として最も適当なものを選びなさい。【内容についての思考力・判断力・表現力】（3点）

   ア. The impact of the film　　　　　イ. The impact of the overfishing

   ウ. The impact of the report　　　　エ. The impact of the survey

3. 下線部(4)とほぼ同じ内容を表す表現を，本文中から抜き出しなさい。

   【内容についての思考力・判断力・表現力の知識】（3点）

   _____

4. 次の問いに英語で答えなさい。【内容についての思考力・判断力・表現力】　　（各4点）

   (1) What was the purpose of the survey?

   _____

   (2) What did most of the audiences say they would do after watching the film?

   _____

A Translate the English into Japanese and the Japanese into English.【語彙の知識】（各1点）

1. ＿＿＿＿＿＿＿ 名 B2　退役軍人，元兵士　　2. renowned 形　[　　　　　　　]

3. director 名 A2　[　　　　　　　]　　4. ＿＿＿＿＿＿＿ 名 B1　ドキュメンタリー

5. injure 動 A2　[　　　　　　　]　　6. ＿＿＿＿＿＿＿ 動 B2　…を始める，…を考案する

B Choose the word whose underlined part is pronounced differently from the other three.【発音の知識】　　　　　　（各2点）

1. ア. injure　　　イ. originate　　　ウ. receive　　　エ. wish

2. ア. about　　　イ. count　　　ウ. renowned　　　エ. snow

3. ア. director　　　イ. letter　　　ウ. senior　　　エ. veteran

C Complete the following English sentences to match the Japanese.【表現と文法の知識】

（各3点）

1. そのイベントは第一次世界大戦の退役軍人のケアをするために開かれた。

The event was held to care for (　　　　　　　　) of World War I.

2. その少年は3年間がんと闘った。

The boy (　　　　　　) (　　　　　　　　) cancer for three years.

3. 父のためのサプライズパーティーの計画は，母が発案した。

My mother (　　　　　　　　) the idea of a surprise party for my father.

D Arrange the words in the proper order to match the Japanese.【表現と文法の知識・技能】

（各3点）

1. 北海道に住んでいる私の友人が来月訪ねてくる。

My friend, (Hokkaido / in / lives / who), is going to visit me next month.

2. その宿題は私には難しすぎたので，兄に助けを求めた。

The homework was too difficult for me, so I (asked / for / help / my brother).

3. 息子は水泳教室に入るまで，一度も泳いだことがなかった。

(had / my son / never / swum) before he joined a swimming class.

E Read the following passage and answer the questions below.

In November 2006, Mitsuru Okoso, the leader of a Japanese NPO group, received a letter from his friend Shoichi Ishida in the U.S. The letter said a group of U.S. war veterans wanted to play softball against some Japanese veterans. (1)They had fought against Japan in World War II.

These veterans, who were all 75 or older, were members of a world-renowned senior softball team in Florida. Ishida was a TV director and had once made a documentary film about the team. One of the veterans (2)(about / for / his wish / Ishida / told) the game, and Ishida then asked Okoso for his help.

(3)(for / originated / the idea / the man / who) the game was Harvey Musser. He had fought against Japan on Leyte Island during the war. He got injured in the left half of his body and lost the sight of his left eye during the battle. He said, "We fought in the war but we do not hate the Japanese. We want to fight with (4)them again, but this time, through a softball game."

1. 下線部(1), (4)が指すものを本文中から抜き出しなさい。【内容についての思考力・判断力・表現力】

(各3点)

(1) ....

(4) ....

2. 下線部(2), (3)の(　　)内の語句を適切に並べかえなさい。【表現の知識】　　(各3点)

(2) ....

(3) ....

3. 次の問いに英語で答えなさい。【内容についての思考力・判断力・表現力】　　(各4点)

(1) How old were the U.S. veterans?

....

(2) Where did Harvey Musser fight against Japan during the war?

....

Bats and Gloves Instead of Bombs and Guns Part 2

/50

A Translate the English into Japanese and the Japanese into English. 【語彙の知識】(各1点)

1. _____ 图 嘆願

2. _____ 图 B1 自殺（行為），決死

3. diver 图 B1 [   ]

4. barely 副 B1 [   ]

5. strengthen 動 B1 [   ]

6. _____ 图 B1 決心，決意

B Choose the word whose underlined part is pronounced differently from the other three. 【発音の知識】(各2点)

1. ア. dec<u>i</u>de   イ. d<u>i</u>ver   ウ. f<u>i</u>nd   エ. <u>i</u>llness

2. ア. ah<u>ea</u>d   イ. l<u>ea</u>flet   ウ. l<u>ea</u>st   エ. pl<u>ea</u>

3. ア. bl<u>ue</u>   イ. h<u>u</u>ge   ウ. l<u>o</u>se   エ. s<u>u</u>icide

C Complete the following English sentences to match the Japanese. 【表現と文法の知識】(各3点)

1. 彼女がその男性の自殺を思いとどまらせた。

   She prevented the man from committing (   ).

2. その選手は勝利への強い決意を示した。

   The player showed his strong (   ) to win.

3. 日々の会話が家族の絆を強くするのにとても重要である。

   Daily conversations are very important to (   ) family bonds.

D Arrange the words in the proper order to match the Japanese. 【表現と文法の知識・技能】(各3点)

1. 伯父さんはもう出発するところだよ。

   Your uncle (about / is / leave / to).

   ----

2. あなたは私の質問に答えていません。

   You (are / my question / not / responding / to).

   ----

3. 彼女がその日に経験したことを誰も知らない。

   No one knows (she / through / went / what) that day.

E Read the following passage and answer the questions below.

Okoso decided to help Ishida and the veterans, and started to look for Japanese senior players. He needed at least 11 players, but it was not an easy job to find (1)them. He set up a website, made a leaflet, and asked newspaper companies and TV stations to report this news. Soon (2)(after / another / one / player / responded) to Okoso's plea.

One player had been a suicide attack diver. He (3)(about / at / die / to / was) the end of the war. (4) had been a pilot who had just barely escaped from an attack by American planes. Still another had experienced an aerial bombing by a B29 and lost many friends. All the players had (5)(go) through that terrible war, but now wanted to enjoy a softball game with Americans.

While gathering the members, Okoso lost two of them as they passed away because of illness. It was a sad experience for him and the other members. However, it strengthened his determination to find a way to successfully hold the game. Finally, he was able to find 19 players.

1. 下線部(1)は何を指していますか。日本語で答えなさい。【内容についての思考力・判断力・表現力】

(2点)

....

2. 下線部(2), (3)の( )内の語を適切に並べかえなさい。【表現の知識】　　(各3点)

(2) ....

(3) ....

3. 空所(4)に入る最も適当な語を選びなさい。【語彙と表現の知識】　　(2点)

ア. Another　　　イ. Other　　　ウ. Others　　　エ. The other

4. 下線部(5)の語を適切な形に変えなさい。【表現と文法の知識】　　(2点)

....

5. 次の問いに英語で答えなさい。【内容についての思考力・判断力・表現力】　　(各4点)

(1) What strengthened Okoso's determination to find a way to successfully hold the game?

....

(2) How many players did Okoso find in the end?

....

Bats and Gloves Instead of Bombs and Guns **Part 3**

/50

A Translate the English into Japanese and the Japanese into English.【語彙の知識】(各1点)

1. _____ 名 B2 真珠　　　　　2. _____ 名 B1 湾

3. overlap 動 [　　　　　　　]　　4. suggest 動 A2 [　　　　　　　]

5. cancel 動 B1 [　　　　　　　]　　6. _____ 名 悪人，悪者

B Choose the word which has primary stress on a different syllable from the other three.【アクセントの知識】　　　　　　　　　　　　　　　　　　　(各2点)

1. ア. at-tack　　　イ. can-cel　　　ウ. oc-cur　　　エ. sug-gest

2. ア. o-ver-lap（動詞）　イ. sta-di-um　　ウ. su-i-cide　　エ. vet-er-an

3. ア. a-vail-a-ble　　イ. con-ven-ient-ly　ウ. dif-fi-cul-ty　エ. ex-pe-ri-ence

C Complete the following English sentences to match the Japanese.【表現と文法の知識】

(各3点)

1. このアプリはこのウェブサイトで入手できる。

   This app is (　　　　　　　) on this website.

2. 翌日になって私は自分が間違っていることがわかった。

   The next day, I (　　　　　　) (　　　　　　) that I was wrong.

3. 春が近づくにつれて，次第に多くの花を道端で見かけるようになる。

   (　　　　　　) spring approaches, I see more and more flowers on the roadside.

D Arrange the words in the proper order to match the Japanese.【表現と文法の知識・技能】

(各3点)

1. 彼は私たちのチームの次のキャプテンになると考えられている。

   He (be / is / thought / to) the next captain of our team.

   _____

2. 私たちは10年前に出会ったが，そのときは2人とも学生だった。

   We met ten years ago, (both / of / us / when) were students.

   _____

3. 生徒の中にはその行事を延期することを提案した者もいた。

   Some students (be / postponed / suggested / that / the event).

   _____

E Read the following passage and answer the questions below.

There were also other tasks for Okoso to do. One was to find a stadium. The location of the game was decided to be in Hawaii as it is warm and conveniently (1)(locate) right between Japan and Florida. Also, it was the place where the attack on Pearl Harbor occurred. Okoso (2)(a stadium / booking / difficulty / had), but finally found one.

Another task was to decide the date. November or December was thought to be the best, as the playing seasons for both sides overlapped during that time. Some U.S. veterans suggested the game be on December 7, when (3)(experienced / had / on / the attack / they) Pearl Harbor in the U.S. time. However, the dates became December 18 and 19 in 2007, when the stadium was available.

As the game was approaching, Okoso found out some of the U.S. members had canceled their participation. One said he didn't feel like (4)(play) with Japanese veterans near Pearl Harbor. Okoso realized that there were still some people in the U.S. who saw the Japanese (5) villains.

1. 下線部 (1), (4)の語を適切な形に変えなさい。【語彙の知識】　　　　　（各2点）

   (1) _____

   (4) _____

2. 下線部(2), (3)の(　　)内の語句を適切に並べかえなさい。【表現の知識】　　（各3点）

   (2) _____

   (3) _____

3. 空所(5)に入る最も適当な語を選びなさい。【語彙と表現の知識】　　　　　（2点）

   ア. as　　　　　　　イ. for　　　　　　　ウ. in　　　　　　　エ. with

4. 次の問いに英語で答えなさい。【内容についての思考力・判断力・表現力】　　（各4点）

   (1) What were the "other tasks" for Okoso?

   _____

   (2) Why didn't the date of the game become December 7?

   _____

Bats and Gloves Instead of Bombs and Guns Part 4

/50

A Translate the English into Japanese and the Japanese into English. 【語彙の知識】(各1点)

1. ＿＿＿＿＿ 名 B2　親善, 友好　　2. ＿＿＿＿＿ 名 B2　戦場

3. heal 動 B1　[　　　　　]　4. wound 名 B1　[　　　　　]

5. ＿＿＿＿＿ 名　イニング, 回　　6. patch 動　[　　　　　]

B Choose the word whose underlined part is pronounced differently from the other three. 【発音の知識】(各2点)

1. ア. b<u>a</u>ttlefield　イ. g<u>a</u>me　ウ. p<u>a</u>st　エ. p<u>a</u>tch

2. ア. c<u>ou</u>ntry　イ. fr<u>o</u>nt　ウ. <u>u</u>nforgettable　エ. w<u>ou</u>nd

3. ア. beh<u>i</u>nd　イ. b<u>ui</u>ld　ウ. goodw<u>i</u>ll　エ. <u>i</u>nning

C Complete the following English sentences to match the Japanese. 【表現と文法の知識】

(各3点)

1. 時間がすべての傷を癒やすと思いますか。

Do you think time (　　　　　) (　　　　　) (　　　　　)?

2. 私は過去のことを忘れようとした。

I tried to put (　　　　　) (　　　　　) (　　　　　) me.

3. その国は反撃できず, 退却を余儀なくされた。

The country could not (　　　　　) (　　　　　) and was forced to retreat.

D Arrange the words in the proper order to match the Japanese. 【表現と文法の知識・技能】

(各3点)

1. 私は最後まで決してあきらめない。

I will never (give / the end / till / up).

＿＿＿＿＿＿＿＿＿＿＿＿＿＿＿＿＿＿＿＿＿

2. 決勝戦はマイアミで行われた。

(held / in / the final / was) Miami.

＿＿＿＿＿＿＿＿＿＿＿＿＿＿＿＿＿＿＿＿＿

3. 彼よりも賢い人なんて思いつかない。

I (anyone / cannot / of / think) who is smarter than him.

＿＿＿＿＿＿＿＿＿＿＿＿＿＿＿＿＿＿＿＿＿

E Read the following passage and answer the questions below.

Play for Goodwill — American and Japanese veterans make runs, not war in Waipahu.

MORE THAN 60 years after WWII, veterans from the US and Japan changed the battlefield into the softball field. Both teams — 14 players from Florida and 19 from Japan — (1)(by / healed / old / playing / wounds) softball together.

The game was held on December 19 in Waipahu, Hawaii. It started with 5 runs by the US team in the 1st inning of the seven-inning game. (2) the Japanese fought back in the 4th and 5th innings, the US led the game till the end. The US (3)(win) with a final score of 14-2.

After the game, Mr. Yasukura, an 84-year-old Japanese veteran, laughed and said, "We (4)(lose) completely, but I enjoyed the game. I'm happy." Mr. Devine, an 82-year-old US veteran, said, "I couldn't think of a better way for people from two countries to patch up old wounds than to play softball together." (5)(both / on / players / teams / used) the game to put the past behind and build an unforgettable friendship.

1. 下線部(1), (5)の(　　)内の語を適切に並べかえなさい。【表現の知識】　　　(各3点)

   (1) ....

   (5) ....

2. 空所(2)に入る最も適当な語を選びなさい。【語彙と表現の知識】　　　(2点)

   ア. But　　　　　イ. However　　　　ウ. If　　　　　エ. Though

3. 下線部(3), (4)の語を適切な形に変えなさい。【語彙の知識】　　　(各2点)

   (3) ....

   (4) ....

4. 次の問いに英語で答えなさい。【内容についての思考力・判断力・表現力】　　　(各4点)

   (1) Where was the game held?

   ....

   (2) Which team scored first?

   ....

A Translate the English into Japanese and the Japanese into English. 【語彙の知識】 (各1点)

1. ＿＿＿＿＿ 名　灌漑　　　2. ＿＿＿＿＿ 名　病床

3. stethoscope 名　[　　　]　　4. capacity 名 B1　[　　　　]

5. catastrophic 形 B2　[　　　]　　6. ＿＿＿＿＿ 名　瀬戸際, 寸前

B Choose the word whose underlined part is pronounced differently from the other three. 【発音の知識】 (各2点)

1. ア. dr<u>ou</u>ght　　イ. <u>o</u>verlap　　ウ. steth<u>o</u>scope　　エ. t<u>o</u>tally

2. ア. d<u>e</u>termination　イ. h<u>ar</u>bor　　ウ. p<u>ear</u>l　　エ. v<u>er</u>ge

3. ア. can<u>a</u>l　　イ. cat<u>a</u>strophic　ウ. exp<u>a</u>nd　　エ. l<u>a</u>ck

C Complete the following English sentences to match the Japanese. 【表現と文法の知識】 (各3点)

1. 暗くなってきたね。もう家に帰る時間だと思うよ。

It's getting dark. I think it's time to head (　　　) home.

2. フレッドは夕食を作っていて手にやけどをした。

Fred burned his hand (　　　) cooking dinner.

3. 私たちは，博物館に入るのに列になって2時間も待たなければいけませんでした。

We had to wait (　　　) (　　　) for two hours to get into the museum.

D Arrange the words in the proper order to match the Japanese. 【表現と文法の知識・技能】 (各3点)

1. 彼は彼女をレストランに残して出て行った。

He went out, (behind / her / in / leaving / the restaurant).

2. 彼はチケット売り場へ急いで行ったが，そのショーのチケットはすでに売り切れていた。

He hurried to the ticket office, (find / for / only / the tickets / to) the show had already been sold out.

3. 私たちはベンチに座って，太陽が丘の向こうに沈むのを眺めました。

We sat on the bench and watched (behind / down / go / the hills / the sun).

E Read the following passage and answer the questions below.

On December 4, 2019, the shocking news of Dr. Tetsu Nakamura's death traveled around the world. Nakamura (1)(a gun attack / dead / in / shot / was) while he was heading for an irrigation canal project site. (2) was the famed Japanese doctor heading for the irrigation canal site, not a hospital?

In 1984, Nakamura was sent (3) Peshawar, Pakistan (4) a physician. Once Nakamura started performing his medical treatment, he realized how limited medical resources were. There were only 16 sickbeds (5) 2,400 patients. Essential medical instruments (6) stethoscopes were totally lacking. He even carried his patients on his back because there were no stretchers in the hospital.

By 1994, Nakamura had established three clinics in Afghanistan to expand his treatment capacity. In 2000, a catastrophic drought struck Afghanistan, leaving four million people on the verge of starvation. (7)(an increasing number / dying children / mothers / of / with) visited Nakamura's clinics, only to see their children lose their lives while waiting in line. Nakamura cried out to himself, "If there were an adequate supply of food and water, these children could survive!"

1. 下線部(1), (7)の(　　)内の語句を適切に並べかえなさい。【表現と文法の知識】　　　（各3点）

(1) _____

(7) _____

2. 空所(2)に入る最も適当な語を選びなさい。【語彙・表現の知識，内容についての思考力・判断力・表現力】

（2点）

　　ア. How　　　　　イ. When　　　　　ウ. Where　　　　エ. Why

3. 空所(3)〜(6)に入る最も適当な語をそれぞれ選びなさい。【語彙の知識】　　　（各1点）

　　ア. as　　　　　　イ. for　　　　　　ウ. like　　　　　エ. to

(3) (　　　　　)　　(4) (　　　　　)　　(5) (　　　　　)　　(6) (　　　　　)

4. 次の問いに英語で答えなさい。【内容についての思考力・判断力・表現力】　　　（各4点）

(1) What did Nakamura realize when he started providing medical treatment in Pakistan?

_____

(2) What could have saved the dying children?

_____

A Translate the English into Japanese and the Japanese into English. 【語彙の知識】（各1点）

1. _____ 動 B1 …を捨てる，…を去る   2. revival 名 B2   [   ]

3. scrape 動   [   ]   4. _____ 形 B2 爆発性の，起爆性の

5. ultimate 形 B2   [   ]   6. _____ 名 B1 目的地

B Choose the word which has primary stress on a different syllable from the other three. 【アクセントの知識】　　　　　　　　　　　　　　　　　　　　　　　（各2点）

1. ア. des-ert　　　　イ. lay-er　　　　ウ. re-store　　　　エ. there-fore

2. ア. a-ban-don　　　イ. ex-plo-sive　　ウ. re-con-struct　　エ. re-viv-al

3. ア. con-tin-u-al　　イ. des-ti-na-tion　ウ. fa-cil-i-ty　　　エ. im-pos-si-ble

C Complete the following English sentences to match the Japanese. 【表現と文法の知識】

（各3点）

1. 彼女はボストンに家を持っているだけでなくニューヨークにアパートを持っている。

She has an apartment in New York as (   ) as a house in Boston.

2. 両腕をばたばたさせて空を飛ぶなんて不可能だ。

It is (   ) to fly by waving your arms.

3. 敵はその工場に爆弾を投下し，吹き飛ばした。

The enemy dropped a bomb on the factory and (   ) it (   ).

D Arrange the words in the proper order to match the Japanese. 【表現と文法の知識・技能】

（各3点）

1. 何であれ，できるようになるためには失敗をするものだ。

You cannot learn to (anything / do / making / mistakes / without).

_____

2. 私たちはレストランを探して1時間歩き回りました。

We walked around (a restaurant / an hour / for / for / looking).

_____

3. 先月注文した商品がまだ届いていない。

The goods (arrived / have / last moth / not / ordered) yet.

_____

E Read the following passage and answer the questions below.

Afghanistan was once a rich agricultural country. However, years of drought as well as continual foreign invasion changed everything. (1)Many villagers could no longer continue farming and had to abandon their villages. Nakamura believed the country would never be reconstructed (2) the revival of the abandoned farmland.

Nakamura and his staff members started to restore dried-up wells and dig new wells. It was impossible to dig deeper into the wells with human hands because of a layer of very large rocks. Therefore, they scraped out explosive materials from unexploded bombs and used them to blow up the rocks. (3) their devoted work, the total number of wells had reached 1,600 (4)(____) 2006.

Nakamura and his members launched the "Green Ground Project." The main part of the project was the construction of a 25-kilometer-long irrigation canal named "Aab-e-Marwarid."

Nakamura had to learn the basics of canal construction. He walked around looking at (5)irrigation facilities (____) only in Afghanistan (____) also in Japan. After seven years of hardship, the canal finally reached its ultimate destination, the Gamberi Desert.

1. 下線部(1)の原因を，日本語で答えなさい。【内容についての思考力・判断力・表現力】　　　（4点）

2. 空所(2)，(3)に入る最も適当な語(句)を選びなさい。【語彙と表現の知識】　　　（各2点）
   (2) ア. by　　　　　イ. unless　　　　ウ. until　　　　エ. without
   (3) ア. According to　イ. In addition to　ウ. Instead of　エ. Thanks to

3. 下線部(4)が「2006年までには」という意味になるように，(　　)に適語を補いなさい。
   【語彙の知識】（2点）

   (　　　　　) 2006

4. 下線部(5)が「アフガニスタンだけでなく日本の用水路設備も」という意味になるように，
   (　　)内に適語を補いなさい。　　　　　　　　　　　【語彙と表現の知識】（2点）

   irrigation facilities (　　　　　) only in Afghanistan (　　　　　) also in Japan

5. 次の問いに英語で答えなさい。【内容についての思考力・判断力・表現力】　　　（各4点）
   (1) What did Nakamura and his staff use to blow up a layer of very large rocks?

   (2) How long did it take to construct the 25-kilometer-long irrigation canal?

/50

A Translate the English into Japanese and the Japanese into English.【語彙の知識】(各1点)

1. .... 名 B1　市民権
2. .... 形　人道主義の
3. tragic 形 B1　[　　　　　　]
4. .... 動 B1　…を悲しむ，…を嘆く
5. spiritually 副　[　　　　　　]
6. livelihood 名　[　　　　　　]

B Choose the word which has primary stress on a different syllable from the other three.【アクセントの知識】(各2点)

1. ア. bright-en　イ. re-gard　ウ. thick-ly　エ. trag-ic
2. ア. in-ci-dent　イ. live-li-hood　ウ. ul-ti-mate　エ. un-der-take
3. ア. cit-i-zen-ship　イ. hon-or-ar-y　ウ. mis-er-a-ble　エ. phi-los-o-phy

C Complete the following English sentences to match the Japanese.【表現と文法の知識】(各3点)

1. 彼女はその国で最高の作家の一人とみなされている。

She is regarded (　　　　　　) one of the best writers in the country.

2. 同時に両方をすることはできません。

You cannot do both at (　　　　) (　　　　) time.

3. あなたの悩みを私たちにお聞かせください。

Please (　　　　　) your problems with us.

D Arrange the words in the proper order to match the Japanese.【表現と文法の知識・技能】(各3点)

1. ロサンゼルスには，女優を目指してウェイトレスとして働く女の子がたくさんいます。

In Los Angeles, (as / many girls / waitresses / work), hoping to become actresses.

2. カメレオンは，体の色を変えるトカゲの一種です。

Chameleons are (a type / changes / lizard / of / which) its body color.

3. 私はその少年たちが木の実をめがけて石を投げているのを見ました。

I saw the boys (at / on / stones / the fruit / throwing) the tree.

E Read the following passage and answer the questions below.

In 2003, Nakamura received the Ramon Magsaysay Award, which is regarded as the Asian version of the Nobel Prize. (1), in 2019, he was granted honorary citizenship by the Afghan government (2) his decades of humanitarian work in the country. In the same year, however, his tragic incident happened. Many people in the world mourned his sudden death. Many Afghans living in Japan gathered to show their deep grief.

Peshawar-kai is an organization which has supported Nakamura's work physically and spiritually. It was established in 1983 to (3)back up his work in Pakistan. After Nakamura's death, it declared it would continue all the work he had undertaken. The local staff regard themselves as the students of the Nakamura school and share his philosophy, "Brighten the world in your corner."

In the Gamberi Desert, which was once feared (4) the desert of death, we can now see trees growing thickly. We can also hear songbirds chirping and frogs croaking. The Aab-e-Marwarid Canal supports the livelihoods of (5)(along / in / 600,000 farmers / the area / the canal) today.

1. 空所(1), (2), (4)に入る最も適当な語(句)を選びなさい。【語彙と表現の知識】　　　　　(各2点)

(1) ア. As a result　　イ. In addition　　ウ. In particular　　エ. Instead

(2) ア. for　　　　　イ. from　　　　　ウ. on　　　　　　エ. to

(4) ア. as　　　　　イ. by　　　　　　ウ. for　　　　　　エ. from

2. 下線部(3)とほぼ同じ意味で用いられる動詞を，本文中から抜き出し原形で答えなさい。

【語彙と表現の知識】（3点）

(　　　　　　　)

3. 下線部(5)の(　　)内の語句を適切に並べかえなさい。【表現の知識】　　　　　　　　（3点）

4. 次の問いに英語で答えなさい。【内容についての思考力・判断力・表現力】　　　　　　（各4点）

(1) After Nakamura's death, what did Peshawar-kai declare?

(2) What did the local staff share after Nakamura's death?

A Translate the English into Japanese and the Japanese into English.【語彙の知識】(各1点)

1. _____ 動 B1 …を捧げる
2. merely 副 B1 [   ]
3. _____ 動 B1 …を建設する
4. directly 副 B1 [   ]
5. _____ 形 B2 立派な, 気高い
6. soul 名 B1 [   ]

B Choose the word which has primary stress on a different syllable from the other three.【アクセントの知識】(各2点)

1. ア. con-struct   イ. main-tain   ウ. no-ble   エ. sup-ply
2. ア. ad-e-quate   イ. ded-i-cate   ウ. di-rect-ly   エ. med-i-cal
3. ア. ca-pac-i-ty   イ. fa-cil-i-ty   ウ. im-pos-si-ble   エ. in-suf-fi-cient

C Complete the following English sentences to match the Japanese.【表現と文法の知識】(各3点)

1. このことは誰にも言わないでね。秘密よ。

   Don't (   ) anyone (   ) this —— it's a secret.
2. 彼は書き上げた本を両親にささげた。

   He (   ) the book he had written (   ) his parents.
3. 火災の際には, エレベーターの代わりに非常階段を利用しなさい。

   In case of fire, use the fire escape (   ) (   ) the elevators.

D Arrange the words in the proper order to match the Japanese.【表現と文法の知識・技能】(各3点)

1. 階段を上り下りすることはよい運動になる。

   (and / down / is / stairs / up / walking) good exercise.

2. パリには1日しかいなかったので, 私はルーブル美術館を訪れる機会はありませんでした。

   Since I was only in Paris for one day, I didn't (get / the chance / the Louvre / to / visit).

3. 彼は仕事を全部自分でしたかのような口ぶりだったが, 実際はその大部分をトムと私がした。

   He talked (all / as / done / had / he / if / the work) himself, but in fact Tom and I did most of it.

E Read the following passage and answer the questions below.

A Japanese famous singer, Masashi Sada, is being interviewed about his newly released song.

Interviewer: Could you tell us about your new song "A grain of wheat —— Moment ——"?

Sada: Yes. I wrote this song to dedicate to Tetsu Nakamura. Many Afghans were suffering from bitter civil wars and devastating droughts. Nakamura worked there as a physician for over thirty years and (1)maintained merely offering medical services was insufficient.

Interviewer: What do you mean (2) "insufficient"?

Sada: Well. Nakamura believed adequate food and water supplies should come (3) medical care. So, he constructed an irrigation canal under the slogan, "One canal instead of 100 clinics."

Interviewer: I see. Have you met Dr. Nakamura before?

Sada: Unfortunately, no. Since I knew some members of Peshawar-kai, I had expected I would see him someday. So I was really shocked to hear that a humanitarian like him was shot dead by an armed group. Though I couldn't have a chance to talk with him directly, I feel as if (4)(had / he / helped / make / me / this song). I strongly believe (5)(Afghanistan / he / in / sowed / the seeds) will continue to grow. We will never forget his kind smile and noble soul.

1. 下線部(1)の意味として，最も適当なものを選びなさい。【語彙の知識】　　　　　　（2点）

　　ア．…を維持する　　　　　イ．…を支持する　　　ウ．…を主張する　　　エ．…を保存する

2. 空所(2)，(3)に入る最も適当な語(句)を選びなさい。【語彙の知識】　　　　　　　（各2点）

　　(2) ア. by　　　　　　　イ. from　　　　　　ウ. for　　　　　　エ. out of

　　(3) ア. after　　　　　　イ. before　　　　　ウ. together　　　　エ. out of

3. 下線部(4)，(5)の(　　)内の語句を適切に並べかえなさい。【表現の知識】　　　　（各3点）

　　(4)　...

　　(5)　...

4. 次の問いに英語で答えなさい。【内容についての思考力・判断力・表現力】　　　　（各4点）

　　(1) Why had Sada expected he would see Nakamura someday?

　　...

　　(2) What happened before Sada could talk directly with Nakamura?

　　...

A Translate the English into Japanese and the Japanese into English.【語彙の知識】(各1点)

1. ＿＿＿＿＿＿＿ 名 B1　栄養　　　　　2. ＿＿＿＿＿＿＿ 名 B1　飢餓, 飢え

3. dietary 形　　　[　　　　　]　　4. vegetarianism 名　　[　　　　　　　]

5. primary 形 B2　[　　　　　]　　6. ＿＿＿＿＿＿＿ 名 B1　流通, 配達

B Choose the word whose underlined part is pronounced differently from the other three.【発音の知識】　(各2点)

1. ア. am<u>ou</u>nt　　イ. c<u>ou</u>nt　　ウ. prof<u>ou</u>nd　　エ. r<u>ou</u>ghly

2. ア. d<u>i</u>etary　　イ. <u>i</u>ndustry　　ウ. pr<u>i</u>mary　　エ. prov<u>i</u>de

3. ア. distrib<u>u</u>tion　　イ. f<u>u</u>ture　　ウ. h<u>u</u>man　　エ. h<u>u</u>nger

C Complete the following English sentences to match the Japanese.【表現と文法の知識】

(各3点)

1. 私たちの学校は新入生一人ひとりにタブレットコンピュータを与えた。

Our school (　　　　　　) each new student (　　　　　　) a tablet PC.

2. 食習慣は国によって大きく異なる。

(　　　　　) (　　　　　　) differ greatly from country to country.

3. その国の子供たちには栄養面の改善が必要だ。

The children in the country need improvements in (　　　　　).

D Arrange the words in the proper order to match the Japanese.【表現と文法の知識・技能】

(各3点)

1. 先月のガス代と電気代は合計で5万円以上になった。

The gas and electricity bills last month (amounted / more / than / to) 50,000 yen.

_____

2. その薬は私の頭痛にはまったく効果がなかった。

The medicine (effect / had / my headache / no / on).

_____

3. 私たちはプラスチックごみに関する諸問題について議論した。

We (related / problems / to / discussed) plastic waste.

_____

E Read the following passage and answer the questions below.

Food is important for our lives.　It provides us with energy and nutrition. However, we have been (1)(face) many serious problems related to food.

For example, the Food and Agriculture Organization (FAO) shows that more than 820 million people, one in every nine on earth, are suffering from hunger. (2) the other hand, the world's annual food waste amounts to 1.3 billion tons. This is roughly a third of the total food production in the world.　(3) addition, many studies report that climate change has had negative effects on crop quality.　Moreover, there is (4)(a / address / growing need / to) the diversity of dietary habits such as vegetarianism and veganism.　Shortages of human resources in primary food-related industries have also been a big challenge for many years.

"Food technology," known as "FoodTech" in Japan, may be one of the promising solutions to many of these problems.　(5)(applying / it / means / science / to) the production, distribution, preparation and development of food. It is expected that the market size of the FoodTech industry will greatly increase in the future.

1. 下線部(1)の語を適切な形に変えなさい。【語彙の知識】　　　　　　　　　　（2点）

　………………………………………………………………………………………

2. 空所(2), (3)に入る最も適当な語をそれぞれ選びなさい。【表現の知識】　　　　（各2点）

　　ア. For　　　　　　　　　イ. In　　　　　　　ウ. On　　　　　　　エ. To

　　(2) (　　　　)　　　　(3) (　　　　)

3. 下線部(4), (5)の(　　)内の語句を適切に並べかえなさい。【表現の知識】　　　　（各3点）

　　(4) …………………………………………………………………………………

　　(5) …………………………………………………………………………………

4. 次の問いに英語で答えなさい。【内容についての思考力・判断力・表現力】　　　　（各4点）

　　(1) According to many studies, what has made crop quality worse?

　　………………………………………………………………………………………

　　(2) What will become of the market size of the FoodTech industry in the future?

　　………………………………………………………………………………………

Food Technology

Part 2

/50

A Translate the English into Japanese and the Japanese into English.【語彙の知識】（各1点）

1. _____ 動 B2 …を利用する
2. chemical 名 B1 [   ]
3. _____ 名 B1 濃度
4. temperature 名 A2 [   ]
5. automatically 副 A2 [   ]
6. _____ 名 光合成

B Choose the word whose underlined part is pronounced differently from the other three.【発音の知識】（各2点）

1. ア. <u>ch</u>aracter　　イ. <u>ch</u>emical　　ウ. ma<u>ch</u>inery　　エ. te<u>ch</u>nology
2. ア. c<u>o</u>ncentration　イ. c<u>o</u>lor　　ウ. <u>o</u>perate　　エ. pr<u>o</u>blem
3. ア. autom<u>a</u>tically　イ. f<u>a</u>med　　ウ. tr<u>a</u>ctor　　エ. v<u>a</u>st

C Complete the following English sentences to match the Japanese.【表現と文法の知識】

（各3点）

1. 山を登るときには急な温度変化に注意しなさい。

When you climb a mountain, be careful with the sudden change in (   ).

2. これらの化学薬品は環境に無害だそうだ。

They say that these (   ) are harmless to the environment.

3. そのドアは自動で閉まる。

The door closes (   ).

D Arrange the words in the proper order to match the Japanese.【表現と文法の知識・技能】

（各3点）

1. この機械は24時間稼働している。

This machine (for / in / is / operation) 24 hours a day.

2. 彼はハンカチに香水をかけた。

He (a handkerchief / perfume / sprayed / with).

3. その少年の話から判断すると，彼の母親はあまり具合が良くないようだ。

(from / judging / says / the boy / what), it seems that his mother is not very well.

E Read the following passage and answer the questions below.

Food technology is utilized in food production in many ways. First, there is now a variety of agricultural machinery. (1), drones are used to spray crops with agricultural chemicals. Remotely operated farm tractors cultivate land. Also, some robots with artificial intelligence harvest crops by judging from their color or shape. These kinds of technology help solve the problem of labor shortages in food production industries.

Second, so-called "plant factories" are now in operation to grow food. They do not need vast land or sunlight. (2)They are not influenced by the weather, either. LED light, CO_2 concentration and temperature in plant factories are automatically controlled for photosynthesis. Plant factories are (3)(an example / deal / of / to / ways) with the problem of climate change.

Food technology is also used in food distribution. For instance, restaurants can reduce food waste by registering for services on the Internet. One service (4)(helps / sell / to / restaurants / their surplus food) general customers at low prices. Such services directly connect food with consumers on the Internet. They are called "D2C" (direct-to-consumer) business models and are only possible through technology.

1. 空所(1)に入る最も適当な語(句)を選びなさい。【語彙と表現の知識】 （3点）

　　ア. For example　　イ. However　　　ウ. In addition　　　エ. On the other hand

2. 下線部(2)が指すものを本文中から抜き出しなさい。【内容についての思考力・判断力・表現力】 （3点）

3. 下線部(3), (4)の（　　）内の語句を適切に並べかえなさい。【表現の知識】 （各3点）

　　(3)

　　(4)

4. 次の問いに英語で答えなさい。【内容についての思考力・判断力・表現力】 （各4点）

　　(1) What do some robots with artificial intelligence do in food production?

　　(2) What are "D2C" business models?

Food Technology

Part 3

/50

A Translate the English into Japanese and the Japanese into English. 【語彙の知識】 (各1点)

1. transform 動 B1　[　　　　　　]　2. ＿＿＿＿＿ 名 B2　物質

3. ＿＿＿＿＿ 名　食感, 舌ざわり　4. liquid 形 B1　[　　　　　　]

5. flavor 名 B1　[　　　　　　]　6. ＿＿＿＿＿ 形 B2　なじみのない

B Choose the word whose underlined part is pronounced differently from the other three. 【発音の知識】 (各2点)

1. ア. <u>a</u>pp　　　イ. fl<u>a</u>vor　　　ウ. t<u>a</u>p　　　エ. tr<u>a</u>nsform

2. ア. contr<u>o</u>l　　イ. gr<u>o</u>cery　　ウ. m<u>ou</u>sse　　エ. ph<u>o</u>tosynthesis

3. ア. <u>a</u>ppliance　イ. d<u>i</u>et　　　ウ. l<u>i</u>quid　　　エ. n<u>i</u>trogen

C Complete the following English sentences to match the Japanese. 【表現と文法の知識】

(各3点)

1. 知らないかもしれないけど, 彼はプロジェクトに貢献してくれました。

You may not know, but he (　　　　　　) (　　　　　　) the project.

2. もっと時間があれば, 私はその問題を解ける。

(　　　　　　) more time, I can solve the problem.

3. 上述のように, その警察官は右腕を負傷しました。

(　　　　　) (　　　　　　) above, the police officer injured her right arm.

D Arrange the words in the proper order to match the Japanese. 【表現と文法の知識・技能】

(各3点)

1. アオムシはどうやって蝶々になるの？

How does a caterpillar (a butterfly / into / itself / transform)?

2. これは実話に基づいた映画です。

This is (a movie / a true story / based / on).

3. このルールは12歳までの子供にしか適用できません。

We can only (apply / children / this rule / to) who are up to 12 years old.

E Read the following passage and answer the questions below.

Food technology also contributes to food preparation. Cooking methods based on food technology have been becoming popular recently. (1), you can transform cooking ingredients into a mousse-formed substance by adding CO_2. This creates different textures. You can also freeze cooking ingredients instantly with liquid nitrogen to preserve their flavor and freshness.

The "smart kitchen" still sounds unfamiliar, but it (2)(change / cook / may / the way / we) at home in the near future. This applies "IoT" (Internet of Things) to cooking. It connects recipes, grocery shopping and food preparation. First, you select your favorite recipe for your meal on a special app in your smartphone. Next, you order the ingredients by tapping on them. Then, after the ingredients are delivered, the smart kitchen will start to help you cook by controlling your kitchen appliances. (3), the smart kitchen can gather various data such as when and what you eat. With such personal data, it (4)(able / be / help / to / will) design an ideal diet.

As mentioned above, food technology is utilized in food preparation in many ways. It will help people enjoy making and eating their meals, and become healthier.

1. 空所(1), (3)に入る最も適当な語句をそれぞれ選びなさい。

【内容についての思考力・判断力・表現力】(各3点)

　　ア. As a result　　イ. For example　　ウ. In addition　　エ. In particular

　　(1) (　　　　　)　　(3) (　　　　　)

2. 下線部(2), (4)の(　　　)内の語句を適切に並べかえなさい。【表現の知識】　　　(各3点)

　　(2)

　　(4)

3. 次の問いに英語で答えなさい。【内容についての思考力・判断力・表現力】　　　(各4点)

　　(1) What can we do by freezing cooking ingredients instantly with liquid nitrogen?

　　(2) How do we order the ingredients when we use the smart kitchen?

A Translate the English into Japanese and the Japanese into English. 【語彙の知識】 (各1点)

1. ＿＿＿＿＿＿ 形 B2　従来の
2. edible 形　[　　　　　　]
3. ＿＿＿＿＿＿ 名 B1　危機
4. nutrient 名 B1　[　　　　　　]
5. ＿＿＿＿＿＿ 名　炭水化物
6. alternative 名 B1　[　　　　　　]

B Choose the word which has primary stress on a different syllable from the other three. 【アクセントの知識】 (各2点)

1. ア. con-sume　　イ. pro-tein　　ウ. soy-bean　　エ. web-page
2. ア. ed-i-ble　　イ. eth-i-cal　　ウ. nu-tri-ent　　エ. re-place-ment
3. ア. al-ter-na-tive　イ. car-bo-hy-drate　ウ. con-ven-tion-al　エ. di-ver-si-ty

C Complete the following English sentences to match the Japanese. 【表現と文法の知識】

(各3点)

1. あなたは，規則は伝統の観点からのみ重要だと言っているのですか。

　Are you saying that the rules are important only (　　　　　　　　)
　(　　　　　) (　　　　　　　　) tradition?

2. 食用の昆虫がいまだに受け入れられない人もいる。

　Some people still cannot accept (　　　　　　　) insects.

3. この牛乳はとても味わい深いチーズへと作りかえられる。

　This milk can be (　　　　　　) (　　　　　　　) very tasty cheese.

D Arrange the words in the proper order to match the Japanese. 【表現と文法の知識・技能】

(各3点)

1. 私たちの家が今そこに建設中です。

　(being / built / is / our house / there) now.

＿＿＿＿＿＿＿＿＿＿＿＿＿＿＿＿＿＿＿＿＿＿＿＿＿＿＿

2. 買う代わりに，市の図書館でたくさん良い本を借りることができるよ。

　You can borrow many good books from the city library (buying / instead / of / them).

＿＿＿＿＿＿＿＿＿＿＿＿＿＿＿＿＿＿＿＿＿＿＿＿＿＿＿

3. 父は怒っていると思っていたが，珍しく上機嫌だった。

　Father was in an unusually good mood, although I (angry / be / expected / him / to).

＿＿＿＿＿＿＿＿＿＿＿＿＿＿＿＿＿＿＿＿＿＿＿＿＿＿＿

E Read the following passage and answer the questions below.

A   Imitation meat and cultured meat

Imitation meat is a meat-like product produced from plants. It is mainly made from soybeans, wheat, peas and so on. (1)It can address dietary diversity such as vegetarianism and veganism. Cultured meat is produced by culturing the cells of animals instead of killing them. Both kinds of meat taste just like real meat, and (2)they may be considered better than conventional meat in terms of ethical, health, environmental, cultural and economic aspects.

B   Insect food

Some insects are edible and high in protein. Actually, (3)(as / been / consumed / have / they) food in some countries for many years. Popular species are grasshoppers, crickets, beetles, bees, and others. Recently, they are being processed with technology and made into various useful forms such as powders, pastes, liquids and oils. Insect food can be mass-produced sustainably and is expected to be a solution to food crises and hunger.

C   Meal replacement

Meal replacement refers to pre-packaged food meals. It is (4)(as / full / nutrients / of / such) proteins, fats, fiber, vitamins, minerals and carbohydrates. It comes in various forms such as powders, bars, drinks, etc. Meal replacement products are convenient alternatives for healthy and low-calorie meals.

1. 下線部(1), (2)は何を指していますか。英語で答えなさい。

【内容についての思考力・判断力・表現力】（各3点）

(1) _____

(2) _____

2. 下線部(3), (4)の(　　)内の語を適切に並べかえなさい。【表現の知識】　　（各3点）

(3) _____

(4) _____

3. 次の問いに英語で答えなさい。【内容についての思考力・判断力・表現力】　　（各4点）

(1) How is cultured meat produced?

_____

(2) In what forms are meal replacement products available?

_____

A Translate the English into Japanese and the Japanese into English.【語彙の知識】（各1点）

1. _____ 形 B1 壊滅的な，破壊的な　　2. _____ 名 B1 貧困

3. blueprint 名　　[　　　　　　　]　　4. tackle 動 B2　　[　　　　　　　]

5. partnership 名 B2　　[　　　　　　]　　6. _____ 名 B1 繁栄

B Choose the word which has primary stress on a different syllable from the other three.【アクセントの知識】（各2点）

1. ア. blue-print　　イ. is-sue　　ウ. trans-form（動詞）　　エ. ur-gent

2. ア. ni-tro-gen　　イ. nu-tri-tion　　ウ. part-ner-ship　　エ. pov-er-ty

3. ア. dev-as-tat-ing　イ. di-e-tar-y　　ウ. pros-per-i-ty　　エ. tem-per-a-ture

C Complete the following English sentences to match the Japanese.【表現と文法の知識】

（各3点）

1. 風がとても強くて，傘をさしているのが難しい。

The wind is (　　　　　　) strong (　　　　　　) it's difficult to hold an umbrella.

2. 私のコンピュータはウイルスに感染しているので，メールを送れないでいます。

My computer has a virus, so I've been (　　　　　　) to send emails.

3. この前の手紙でお知らせしたように，私は7月に試験を受けます。

(　　　　　　) I said in my last letter, I am taking the exam in July.

D Arrange the words in the proper order to match the Japanese.【表現と文法の知識・技能】

（各3点）

1. 私が勤めている会社は，パリとミラノとニューヨークに支店があります。

The company (branches / for / has / I / work) in Paris, Milan and New York.

2. できるだけ早くあなたの結論をお知らせください。

Please (as / know / let / me / your decision) soon as possible.

3. 民主主義は，社会を構成するすべての人は平等であるという考えに基づいている。

Democracy is based on (all members / of / society / that / the idea) are equal.

E Read the following passage and answer the questions below.

Now, (1)(　　) me give you three examples of global issues facing the world today. First, we often hear news like "We had the most devastating flood in a century." In fact, climate change has become so serious that it can (2)be referred to (　　) the "climate crisis." Second, unfortunately, hunger and poverty in developing countries still remain as huge barriers to sustainable development. According to the United Nations, every year about six million children die from hunger and poor nutrition. The third example is the issue of education. We have to face the (　3　) that hundreds of millions of children around the world are unable to attend school.

As you know, there is (4)(in / lose / no time / tackling / to) these global issues. That's why the UN has adopted the 17 Sustainable Development Goals — the SDGs. They are a blueprint for peace and prosperity for people and the planet, now and into the future. They are an urgent call to action by all countries in a global partnership.

Now is the time to consider what we can do as individuals. It is not enough (5)(for / to / understand / us / what) the issues are. We must transform the world through our daily actions.

1. 下線部(1)が「3つの例を挙げさせてください」という意味に，下線部(2)が「…と言及される」という意味になるように，(　)に適語を補いなさい。【語彙と表現の知識】　　　（各2点）

(1) (　　　　　) me give you three examples

(2) be referred to (　　　　　) …

2. 空所(3)に入る最も適当な語を選びなさい。【表現の知識】　　　　　　　　　（2点）

ア. belief　　　　　イ. fact　　　　　ウ. news　　　　　エ. opinion

3. 下線部(4)，(5)の(　)内の語(句)を適切に並べかえなさい。【表現と文法の知識】　　　（各3点）

(4) _____

(5) _____

4. 次の問いに英語で答えなさい。【内容についての思考力・判断力・表現力】　　　（各4点）

(1) How many children die each year from hunger and poor nutrition?

_____

(2) What do the SDGs call for?

_____

A Translate the English into Japanese and the Japanese into English. 【語彙の知識】 (各1点)

1. _____ 名 B2 協力

2. _____ 名 B1 目標, 目的

3. illiterate 形 [   ]

4. cycle 名 B1 [   ]

5. harsh 形 [   ]

6. _____ 名 読み書きができないこと

B Choose the word whose underlined part is pronounced differently from the other three. 【発音の知識】 (各2点)

1. ア. en<u>a</u>ble   イ. esc<u>a</u>pe   ウ. <u>o</u>bjective   エ. pl<u>a</u>net

2. ア. h<u>ar</u>sh   イ. p<u>ar</u>tnership   ウ. ref<u>er</u>   エ. st<u>ar</u>vation

3. ア. d<u>e</u>cent   イ. <u>i</u>lliterate   ウ. p<u>ea</u>   エ. prot<u>ei</u>n

C Complete the following English sentences to match the Japanese. 【表現と文法の知識】 (各3点)

1. この箱を私一人では動かせません。手伝ってくれませんか。

I can't move this box on my (   ). Can you help me?

2. 毎年とてもたくさんの観光客がこの博物館を訪れます。

(   ) large (   ) of tourists visit this museum every year.

3. その農場は彼らが必要とする食料をすべて提供した。

The farm provided them (   ) all the food they needed.

D Arrange the words in the proper order to match the Japanese. 【表現と文法の知識・技能】 (各3点)

1. 彼は, 車いすの人が階段を上れるようにするある機械を発明した。

He invented a machine (in / people / to enable / to go / wheelchairs) up stairs.

2. シンディーの歌にとても感動したので, 彼は彼女にテレビで歌ってくれるように頼んだ。

He (by / Cindy's singing / impressed / so / was) that he asked her to sing on TV.

3. 人々は, 政治家たちが守りもしない約束をするのを聞くのにうんざりしている。

People are tired (hearing / make / of / politicians / promises) that they never keep.

E Read the following passage and answer the questions below.

I'd like to talk about SDG Goal 4, "Quality Education." I think education is the most important thing to improve our society. This SDG's goal is to (1)(　　) sure that everyone can equally get a good education. Education enables us to live on our own and escape poverty. I have learned that a large number of children around the world cannot attend school. I'm very shocked to know (2)this reality. (3)I'm (　　) what we can do as individuals.

I want to introduce the "World TERAKOYA Movement (WTM)." In 1989, a Japanese NGO started it as an international cooperation program for education. The main objective of the WTM is to provide illiterate adults and out-of-school children with opportunities to receive an education. I am impressed by the goal of the WTM: to end (4)the cycle of poverty and illiteracy.

On its website, I heard a TERAKOYA student say, "I'm very happy that I was able to write my name (　5　) in my life." My future dream is to be a teacher. I hope to teach children living in harsh conditions like him someday.

1. 下線部(1)が「…を確実にする」, 下線部(3)が「…は何だろうかと思っている」という意味になるように, (　　)に適語を補いなさい。【語彙と表現の知識】　　　　　　　　　　(各2点)

   (1) (　　　　　　　　) sure that …

   (3) I'm (　　　　　　　　) what …

2. 下線部(2), (4)の具体的な内容を, 日本語で答えなさい。【内容についての思考力・判断力・表現力】

                                                 (各3点)

   (2) _____

   (4) _____

3. 空所(5)に入る最も適当な語句を選びなさい。【表現の知識】　　　　　　　　　　(2点)

   ア. at first　　　　　　　　　　　　　　イ. first of all

   ウ. for the first time　　　　　　　　　エ. from the first

4. 次の問いに英語で答えなさい。【内容についての思考力・判断力・表現力】　　　　　(各4点)

   (1) Why does Manabu think education is the most important thing to improve society?

   _____

   (2) Who are learning at TERAKOYA schools?

   _____

Transforming Our World

Part 3

/50

A Translate the English into Japanese and the Japanese into English. 【語彙の知識】(各1点)

1. _____ 形 B1 信頼できる   2. _____ 名 B1 燃料

3. renewable 名 [   ]   4. _____ 名 水力発電

5. shift 動 B1 [   ]   6. source 名 A2 [   ]

B Choose the word which has primary stress on a different syllable from the other three. 【アクセントの知識】

(各2点)

1. ア. fos-sil   イ. pre-serve   ウ. pro-duce(動詞)   エ. pro-vide

2. ア. de-vel-op   イ. en-er-gy   ウ. ob-jec-tive   エ. po-ten-tial

3. ア. af-ford-a-ble   イ. gen-er-a-tion   ウ. re-li-a-ble   エ. re-new-a-ble

C Complete the following English sentences to match the Japanese. 【表現と文法の知識】

(各3点)

1. ウールは羊から取れる。

   Wool (   ) from sheep.

2. 彼のプレゼンテーションは，大部分はとてもよかった。

   His presentation was, (   ) the most (   ), pretty good.

3. すぐに行動を起こさないと手遅れになるぞ。

   If we don't (   ) action now, it'll be too late.

D Arrange the words in the proper order to match the Japanese. 【表現と文法の知識・技能】

(各3点)

1. 疲れているようだね。きみには休暇が必要だ。

   You look tired. (a vacation / is / need / what / you).

2. 以前どこかでお会いしましたよね？

   (haven't / met / somewhere / we) before?

3. たとえどんなに遅くなっても，着いたら電話をしてくれ。

   Call me when you arrive, no (how / is / it / late / matter).

E Read the following passage and answer the questions below.

What I am most interested in is SDG Goal 7. Its purpose is to provide people with affordable, reliable, sustainable and clean energy. For many years, fossil fuels have been the major energy resource. But burning fossil fuels has been producing large amounts of greenhouse gases. (1)They have caused climate change and have had harmful impacts (2) the environment.

Let me tell you about Norway. Surprisingly, in Norway, almost 100% of all electricity production comes from renewables, for the most part hydropower. Norway's energy policy may be a special case, (3) it's a good model for our country. As you know, Japan is trying to increase the use of renewables, but their percentage will only increase from 18% to over 30% by 2030.

Don't you think it is time to take urgent action to shift (4) fossil fuels (5) renewables? However, the world, especially many developing countries, will need more and more energy to develop their economies. It is a great challenge to meet all the potential energy needs only by using clean energy sources. No matter how difficult (6)it is, we must do it to preserve the earth for future generations.

1. 下線部(1)は何を指していますか。英語で答えなさい。【内容についての思考力・判断力・表現力】（3点）

2. 空所(2), (3)に入る最も適当な語を選びなさい。【語彙の知識】 （各2点）

   (2) ア. for   イ. in   ウ. of   エ. on

   (3) ア. and   イ. but   ウ. or   エ. so

3. 空所(4), (5)に入る最も適当な語をそれぞれ選びなさい。【語彙の知識】 （完答2点）

   ア. from   イ. into   ウ. out   エ. to

   (4) (   )   (5) (   )

4. 下線部(6)は何を指していますか。日本語で答えなさい。【内容についての思考力・判断力・表現力】

（3点）

5. 次の問いに英語で答えなさい。【内容についての思考力・判断力・表現力】 （各4点）

   (1) What is Norway's electricity production mainly dependent on?

   (2) What percentage of Japan's electricity production today comes from renewables?

A Translate the English into Japanese and the Japanese into English. 【語彙の知識】（各1点）

1. .... 名 B2 医療
2. .... 形 B1 極度の，極端な
3. fulfill 動 B2 [   ]
4. border 名 B1 [   ]
5. epidemic 名 [   ]
6. .... 副 B1 きっと，確実に

B Choose the word which has primary stress on a different syllable from the other three. 【アクセントの知識】 （各2点）

1. ア. en-sure   イ. ex-treme   ウ. ful-fill   エ. health-care
2. ア. dis-as-ter   イ. per-cent-age   ウ. po-ten-tial   エ. vol-un-teer
3. ア. ar-ti-fi-cial   イ. def-i-nite-ly   ウ. ep-i-dem-ic   エ. pol-i-ti-cian

C Complete the following English sentences to match the Japanese. 【表現と文法の知識】

（各3点）

1. その町には仕事がほとんどなく，多くの人が貧しい生活をしていました。

   There were very few jobs in the town, and many people lived (   ) poverty.

2. ボルネオにあるオランウータンの学校のことを聞いたことがありますか。

   Have you (   ) heard (   ) schools for orangutans in Borneo?

3. できれば，あなたの返事を今日聞かせてもらえませんか。

   (   ) (   ), could you give me your answer today?

D Arrange the words in the proper order to match the Japanese. 【表現と文法の知識・技能】

（各3点）

1. あなたからいただいたこの素晴らしい機会を，喜んでお受けいたします。

   I (accept / be / happy / this / to / would) wonderful opportunity you have given me.

2. 委員会はすべての政党の政治家で構成されている。

   The committee is (from / made / of / politicians / up) all parties.

3. どの車も登録番号を表記したナンバープレートを付けなければならない。

   Every car must have (a license plate / it / its registration number / on / with).

E Read the following passage and answer the questions below.

I'd like to take up SDG Goal 1 and SDG Goal 3. SDG Goal 1, "No Poverty," is to end (1)poverty (   ) all its forms everywhere by 2030. SDG Goal 3, "Good Health and Well-being," aims to ensure healthy lives and promote well-being for all people of all ages.

SDG Goals 1 and 3 are strongly interconnected. (2), "No Poverty" is closely linked to good health. (3), people living in extreme poverty cannot fulfill their most basic needs like good health. Have you ever heard of "Doctors Without Borders"? It is an international medical humanitarian organization founded in 1971 in Paris. It provides (4)(affected / basic / by / for / medical care / people) war, epidemics or disasters. I am impressed that it is trying to realize SDG Goals 1 and 3.

My future dream, if possible, is to work as a volunteer for "Doctors Without Borders." The organization is made up (5)(diverse backgrounds / from / of / people / with) all over the world. The experience of working with such people would definitely be a precious opportunity for me, and I would be happy to contribute to the achievement of the goals of the SDGs.

1. 下線部(1)が「あらゆる形態の貧困」という意味になるように，（   ）に適語を補いなさい。

【語彙と表現の知識】（ 2 点）

poverty (   ) all its forms

2. 空所(2), (3)に入る最も適当な語句を選びなさい。【語彙と表現の知識】 （各 2 点）

(2) ア. As a result　　イ. In addition　　ウ. In other words　　エ. In particular

(3) ア. If possible　　イ. In addition　　ウ. In conclusion　　エ. In fact

3. 下線部(4), (5)の（   ）内の語句を適切に並べかえなさい。【表現と文法の知識】 （各 3 点）

(4) _____

(5) _____

4. 次の問いに英語で答えなさい。【内容についての思考力・判断力・表現力】 （各 4 点）

(1) What is "Doctors Without Borders" trying to do?

_____

(2) What does Vivian want to do by working for "Doctors Without Borders"?

_____